How to Prepare
For the CAT/6*

* SAT9 is a registered trademark of Harcourt Brace, which was not involved in the production of and does not endorse this product.

8th Grade Edition
By Bob Huson
Dale Lundin
Nancy Samuels

CARNEY EDUCATIONAL SERVICES
Helping Students Help Themselves

Special thanks to Rim Namkoong, our illustrator

This book is dedicated to:

The moms and dads who get up early and stay up late. You are the true heroes, saving our future, one precious child at a time.

All the kids who don't make the evening news. To the wide-eyed children, full of love, energy, and wonder. You are as close to perfection as this world will ever see.

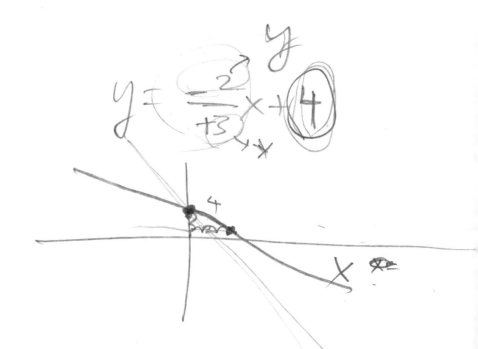

TABLE OF CONTENTS

8th Grade Edition

An Overview of the CAT/6 Test

In the spring of 2002, the California Department of Education adopted the California Achievement Test, Sixth Edition (the CAT/6) as part of the state's Standardized Testing and Reporting System (STAR). The purpose behind this test is to provide California public school districts and parents with information about how their children are performing compared with other public school children from across the state. Keep in mind that this is a test of basic skills. It was written to assess the abilities of students only in specified areas of the curriculum. The CAT/6 is a standardized test, meaning that all public school children across California take the tests in the same manner and during the same months of the school year period. The directions given by teachers are the same, as are the amounts of time given to complete each testing section.

Why did California change from the SAT 9 to the CAT/6?

Over the last several years, the Stanford 9 (also referred to as SAT 9) standardized tests had generated controversy in some school districts due to errors in data analysis. Some of the important information reported by school districts was misused or analyzed incorrectly. These errors became quite costly to identify and correct. Additionally, some districts with large numbers of non-English speaking students encouraged parents to request waivers which would exclude their children from taking the SAT 9. Obviously, districts which sought to exclude such students from taking the test would receive higher scores than those districts which sought to test every student. In changing to the CAT/6, the California Board of Education decided to use a test with much more of a history in the state. The California Aptitude Tests were first developed in 1950, and are currently in use in nine other states. The CAT/6 will be administered by the Educational Testing Service (ETS), which is the largest testing firm in the nation.

What does the CAT/6 seek to measure?

Beginning in the spring of 2003, approximately 4.5 million students in grades 2-11 will be taking multiple choice tests in two main areas of the curriculum: Mathematics and Language Arts. The specific skills tested within Language Arts are vocabulary, reading comprehension, spelling, language mechanics (grammar), and language expression (word usage). The math sections of the test measure student mastery of math computation, math concepts and math applications. Students in grades 4-12 may be given a study skills subtest, which will measure how well student scan use information processing skills which they can use across all subject areas. The CAT test series also contains science and social studies subtests, but whether these will be used as part of the STAR program has yet to be determined.

Why do schools give standardized tests?

The CAT/6 gives schools an idea of how well they are teaching basic skills which all students need to be successful in the future. These skills are defined for schools in documents called "State Standards." The State Department of Education has spelled out for teachers, parents and students what they should be learning in each academic subject during a given school year. Schools receive data about how their students performed both individually and by grade level. Which state standards did students meet? Which standards need to be taught differently next year? How can schools help each child move toward meeting all the standards? All of these questions can be best answered by using the data provided by the CAT/6. Standardized tests are valuable because they are an objective way to measure how successfully schools are delivering the basics. The idea behind standardizing the test is this: if every public school student takes the same tests in the same way, then it is a fair way to compare schools and districts. If, for example, one school gave children an extra 5 hours to complete the test, then it would be an unfair advantage given to those children.

What about criticism of standardized tests?

In the last few years, criticism of standardized tests has mounted. Many parents and teachers say that preparing for these tests takes away time from valuable subjects like art, drama and music. They have also noted the stressful nature of these tests and question whether it is healthy to subject young children to this type of pressure to perform. Others believe these tests reward wealthy school districts in the suburbs, while they punish inner-city school districts with large numbers of non-English speaking students. While some of these criticisms are valid, they do not change the fact that standardized tests are widely regarded as the best way for schools to measure how they are teaching to the California State Standards. As long as the public asks public schools to prove they are doing an effective job educating children, these tests will be with us. The criticism of the Stanford 9 test resulted in replacing it with the CAT/6, which is ANOTHER standardized test.

As parents, we need to realize that these tests have become a fact of life in California public schools and help children prepare for them. Certainly, schools and teachers are primarily responsible for preparing your child for these tests. Yet parents have an important role to play. This book will give you many valuable tools you can use in helping your child do their best on this very important standardized test. It is the job of California public schools to teach to the standards, which are tested on the CAT/6, but your role as a reinforcer of skills and a supporter of your child's progress as a student cannot be ignored.

How Your Child Can Improve His/Her Score On ANY
Multiple Choice Standardized Test

Your child has entered an educational world that is run by standardized tests. Students take the Scholastic Aptitude Test (SAT) to help them get into college and the Graduate Record Examination (GRE) to help them get into graduate school. Other exams like the ACT and the PSAT are not as well-known, but also very important to your child's future success. Schools spend a great deal of time teaching children the material they need to know to do well on these tests, but very little time teaching children HOW to take these tests. This is a gap that parents can easily fill. To begin with, you can look for opportunities to strengthen your child's reading and vocabulary skills as well as his/her ability to follow detailed written directions.

The importance of reading:

Students who do well on standardized tests tend to be excellent readers. They read frequently for pleasure and have a good understanding of what they have read. You can help support your child as a reader by helping him/her set aside a regular time to read each and every day. As you may know, children tend to be successful when they follow an established pattern of behavior. Even 15-20 minutes spent reading a magazine or newspaper before bedtime will help. Children should read both fiction and non-fiction material at home, as well as at school. Ask your child about what s/he has read. Help him/her to make connections between a book s/he is currently reading and a movie or a television show s/he has recently seen. THE BOTTOM LINE: Children who read well will do better on the test than children who do not. There is written material in all sections of the test that must be quickly comprehended. Even the math sections have written information contained in each question.

The importance of building a larger vocabulary:

As you may know, children who read well and who read often tend to have a large vocabulary. This is important since there is an entire section of the test that is devoted exclusively to the use of vocabulary words. You can support your child in attempting to improve his/her vocabulary by encouraging him/her to read challenging material on a regular basis. The newspaper is a good place to start. Studies have shown that many newspaper articles are written on a 4th to 5th grade reading level! Help your child to use new and more difficult words both in his/her own conversations and in his/her writings. If you use an advanced vocabulary when speaking to your children, don't be surprised if they begin to incorporate some of the new words into his/her daily speech. One of the most immediate ways to judge the intelligence of anyone is in his/her use of language. Children are aware of this too. THE BOTTOM LINE: Children who have an expansive vocabulary will do better on the test than children who do not. Find as many ways as possible to help build new words into your child's speech and writing.

The importance of following written directions:

The test is a teacher-directed test. Teachers tell students how to complete each section of the test and give them specific examples that are designed to help them understand what to do. However, teachers are not allowed to help students once each test has begun. The written script for teachers seems to repeat one phrase continually: "READ THE DIRECTIONS CAREFULLY." This is certainly not an accident. Students face a series of questions that cannot be answered correctly unless they clearly understand what is being asked. Help your child by giving him/her a series of tasks to complete at home in writing. Directions should be multi-step and should be as detailed as possible without frustrating your child. For example: "Please take out the trash cans this afternoon. Place all the bottles and cans in the blue recycling bin and place all the extra newspapers that are stacked in the garage in the yellow recycling bin." If children are able to follow these types of directions and are able to reread to clarify what is being asked, they will be at a tremendous advantage when it comes to the test.
THE BOTTOM LINE: Children who are able to follow a series of detailed, written directions will have a tremendous advantage over those who are unable to do so.

All of the previous suggestions are designed to be used before the test is actually given to help your child improve in some basic test-taking skills. Here are some strategies that you can teach your child to use once s/he is taking the test:

1. SELECT THE BEST ANSWER.

The test, like many multiple-choice tests, isn't designed for children to write their own answers to the questions. They will fill in a bubble by the four answer choices and select the BEST possible answer. Reading the question carefully is quite important, since the question may contain key words needed to select the correct answer. For example:

The first President of the United States was

a. John Adams.
b. James Madison.
c. George Washington.
d. Thomas Jefferson.

The correct answer is, of course, "c". Students would need to read the question carefully and focus on the key word in the question: "first". All of the names listed were Presidents of the United States early in our history, but only choice "c" contains the name of our first President. Looking for key words like "least" or "greater" will help your child to select the best answer from among the choices given.

2. ANSWER THE EASY QUESTIONS FIRST.

The test contains a series of timed tests. Children who waste time on a difficult question found at the beginning of a test may run out of time before they finish the entire test. A good strategy is to skip anything that seems too difficult to answer immediately. Once your children have answered every "easy" question in the section, they can go back through the test and spend more time working on the more time-consuming questions. If students are given only 30 minutes to answer 25 reading vocabulary questions, they shouldn't spend much more than a minute on each one. Wasting four or five minutes on one question is not a good idea, since it reduces the amount of time your child will have to work on the rest of the test. Once time runs out, that's it! Any questions left unanswered will be counted wrong when the test is machine scored. Working on the easier questions first will allow your child to make the best use of the allowed time.

3. ELIMINATE ANY UNREASONABLE ANSWER CHOICES.

No matter how intelligent your child is, it is inevitable that s/he will come to a test question that s/he finds too difficult to answer. In this situation, the best thing to do is to make an "educated guess." If students can eliminate one or more of the answer choices given, they have a much greater chance of answering the question correctly.

For example:

Select the word below that means the same as the underlined word:

Jennifer became <u>enraged</u> when she found out her diary had been read.

   a. mournful
   b. furious
   c. pleased
   d. depressed

Even if your child didn't know that "b" is the best answer choice, s/he could certainly eliminate choice "c" from consideration. Clearly, Jennifer would not be "pleased" to find out her diary had been read.

4. DO MATH QUESTIONS ON PAPER WHEN NECESSARY.

The math sections of the test cause children problems because several of the answer choices seem like they could be correct. The only way to select the best answer choice for some math questions is to do the math calculation on scratch paper. The answer choices given for these questions are written to discourage guessing.

For example:

Eileen has saved $3245 to buy a car. Her aunt gave her another $250 as a gift. How much does she have in all?

    a. $3595
    b. $4495
    c. $3495
    d. $3485

The correct answer is "c", but it is hard to select the correct answer because all of the answer choices seem similar. The best way to determine the correct answer would be to add $3245 and $250 on scratch paper.

> If you work with your children with these simple strategies, you will find that they will approach these tests with confidence, rather than with anxiety. Teach your children to prepare and then to approach the test with a positive attitude. They should be able to say to themselves, "I know this stuff, I'll do a great job today."

LANGUAGE ARTS

Content Cluster: WORD ANALYSIS AND VOCABULARY DEVELOPMENT

Objectives: To evaluate the student's understanding of: (1) the meaning of grade-level-appropriate words; (2) the use of idioms, analogies, metaphors, and similes to infer meaning; (3) the history of the English language and common word origins; and (4) the use of historical and literary context clues to enhance comprehension of written material.

Parent Tip: As part of the State Academic Content Standards for Reading in Grade 8, students are expected to use their knowledge of word origins, word relationships, and context clues, to understand the precise meaning of words that they encounter in literature and content area textbooks. The more one reads, the more one becomes proficient at the task. Using a dictionary to determine the meanings of new words is essential, but a good reader also tries to work out the word's meaning by analyzing the context in which it appears. So, encourage your child to read newspapers, magazines, novels, poetry—some printed material—every day. When she encounters an unknown word or phrase, she can practice analyzing the words that come before it and after it to get an idea of the sentence meaning. Then make a prediction of the word's meaning by reading more of the passage. Finally, look it up in the dictionary and write down the meaning in a notebook. Many people find it easier to remember the word's meaning if they also write the sentence in which they first encountered the word. A powerful vocabulary building strategy is to use the word as often as possible in speaking and writing in order to commit it to long-term memory.

In exercises 1 - 25, based on the context provided within the sentence or passage, select the word(s) closest in meaning to the underlined word.

Example A:

A traffic sign should be <u>conspicuous</u>.

      a. hidden
      b. easily seen
      c. invisible
      d. noteworthy

The answer is choice *b, easily seen*. If you did not know the meaning of the underlined word, or if (as in the case of the example) the underlined word has multiple meanings that are among the choices given, consider using one of the following strategies. First, substitute each of the choices for the underlined word and reread the sentence each time. Does the new sentence make sense? In the above example, this would automatically eliminate choices *a* and *c*, because hidden or invisible traffic signs would serve no purpose at all. Although *noteworthy* is a synonym for *conspicuous,* it would fit better in the context of another sentence, such as "Abraham Lincoln is a conspicuous example of a poor child who achieved great success." By process of elimination, you have chosen the correct answer, *easily seen.*

Next, analyze the structure of the sentence to see if it gives you any clues about word meaning. Try this in Example B.

Example B:

Rupert routinely went to bed at 7:30, fell asleep quickly, and enjoyed peaceful slumber throughout the night; but last night he experienced <u>insomnia</u>.

    a. praise
    b. deep sleep
    c. fatigue
    d. inability to sleep

The answer is choice *d, inability to sleep.* If you did not know the meaning of the underlined word, the substitution strategy would help you eliminate choice *a, praise,* because the new sentence doesn't make any sense. In addition, you could look at the structure of the sentence for clues as to meaning. The word *but* signals that two parts of the sentence contrast each other, and that you should look for a word that conveys the opposite meaning from the first part of the sentence. Therefore, you can eliminate choices *b* and *c, deep sleep* and *fatigue,* because they support the idea conveyed in the first part of the sentence. That reasoning leads you to the correct choice, *d.* The exercises that follow are designed to give you practice using context clues to construe meaning. If a single exercise contains several words that require definition, read through the entire passage one time from beginning to end in order to get a sense of its overall meaning; then return to the task of finding the meaning of selected words.

1. The old cabin was <u>habitable</u>, although the roof needed patching in one place.

    a. in need of repair
    b. fit to live in
    c. routine
    d. round

The frontier, the <u>sparsely</u> populated (not more than six to the square mile) border area of America in the early 1800s, had a <u>profound</u> impact on the character of our people. It ensured that individual <u>initiative</u> would be the <u>heritage</u> of generations of Americans. Those who ventured into the frontier demonstrated to a new nation that they were ready, willing, and able to lead the western movement. The earliest hunters and trappers lived in miserable <u>hovels</u>, which they <u>fortified</u> when they fought with the Native Americans. They <u>paved the way</u>, <u>albeit</u> ever so slightly, for the next wave of settling pioneers who were similarly daring folks. Although unpolished, they were <u>hospitable</u> and kind to strangers. They were <u>extraordinarily</u> hard workers, for they had to clear the land, build family homes, grow their own grain, vegetables, and fruit, and hunt in the woods or fish the streams for more food. The more <u>enterprising</u> pioneers bought some extra land, then resold it when land values rose, only to start again, <u>lock stock, and barrel</u>, farther west!

2. sparsely

   a. heavily
   b. thinly scattered
   c. troubled
   d. effortlessly

3. profound

   a. doubtful
   b. touchy
   c. very deep
   d. only slight

4. initiative

   a. taking the first step or move
   b. stopping
   c. wanting
   d. adoring

5. heritage

   a. what is handed on to people by their ancestors
   b. postage
   c. debt
   d. understanding

6. hovels

   a. safe forts
   b. mansions
   c. comfort
   d. small, unpleasant dwellings

7. fortified

   a. abandoned
   b. hid
   c. strengthened
   d. destroyed

8. paved the way

    a. cemented roads
    b. drove through
    c. prepared the way
    d. hesitated

9. albeit

    a. not
    b. entirely
    c. without
    d. although

10. hospitable

    a. friendly toward guests
    b. unwelcoming
    c. sick
    d. frightening

11. extraordinarily

    a. regularly
    b. most remarkably
    c. occasionally
    d. quite surprisingly

12. enterprising

    a. entertaining
    b. confused and befuddled
    c. full of enthusiasm and initiative
    d. lazy

13. lock, stock, and barrel

    a. with guns and ammunition
    b. in a warlike manner
    c. without enthusiasm
    d. entirely, the whole thing

"We regard ourselves as happy under Great Britain's rule. We love, esteem, and <u>revere</u> our mother country, and honor our king. If the colonies were offered a choice between independence and <u>subjection</u> to Great Britain upon any <u>terms</u> other than absolute slavery, I am convinced they would accept <u>subjection</u>. The British government in all future <u>generations</u> may be sure that the American colonies will never try to leave Britain's rule unless driven to it as the last desperate action against <u>oppression</u>. It will be an <u>oppression</u> that will make the wisest person mad and the weakest strong...."

-James Otis, from "The Rights of the British Colonies Asserted and Proved"
Source: <u>The Story of America</u>, by John A Garrity

14. revere
    a. hate
    b. highly resent
    c. deeply respect
    d. reject

15. subjection
    a. being under the control or influence of
    b. understanding
    c. learning or studying
    d. freedom

16. terms
    a. length of time
    b. rumor or gossip
    c. friendship
    d. conditions

17. generations
    a. military actions
    b. genuine advice
    c. people born in a period of time
    d. machines

18. oppression
    a. unlimited freedom
    b. cruel or unjust government
    c. opportunity to improve
    d. opposite view

19. asserted
    a. firmly declared
    b. questioned
    c. destroyed
    d. negated

"I wish you, Sir, to believe, that it may be understood in America, that I have done nothing in the late contest but what I thought myself indispensably bound to do by the duty which I owed my people. I will be very frank with you. I was the last to consent to the separation; but the separation having been made, and having become inevitable, I have always said, as I say now, that I would be the first to meet the friendship of the United States as an independent power."

    -King George III of England, in a message of peace to John Adams after the
    Revolutionary War
      Source: The Story of America, by John A Garrity

20. late contest
    a. recent war
    b. games played after dinner
    c. House of Lords
    d. Royal gardens

21. indispensably
    a. indiscreetly
    b. without power
    c. possibly
    d. absolutely and necessarily

22. frank
    a. dishonest and equivocal
    b. candid and outspoken
    c. disrespectful
    d. untruthful and cunning

23. consent
    a. argue about
    b. politely offer
    c. agree or give approval
    d. disagree or argue against

24. inevitable
    a. unavoidable, sure to happen
    b. impossible
    c. doubtful
    d. ineligible

25. meet
    a. to fight with
    b. to acknowledge, connect with
    c. to deny
    d. to question

Select the answer that best completes the sentence.

In the first issue of *The Liberator*, abolitionist William Lloyd Garrison wrote, "I *will be* as harsh as truth, and as ___[26]___ as justice. . . . I am in earnest--I will not ___[27]___ --I will not excuse--I will not ___[28]___ a single inch--And *I WILL BE HEARD!*" Could anyone question his ___[29]___? Even after other leaders of the abolition movement turned against him, Garrison remained a tireless, ___[30]___ ___[31]___ for the antislavery cause.

26.
    a. uncompromising
    b. undecided
    c. acidic
    d. foolish

27.
    a. remember
    b. wonder
    c. equivocate
    d. proceed

28.
    a. work
    b. retreat
    c. forget
    d. proceed

29.
    a. mastery
    b. resolve
    c. rejection
    d. collection

30.
    a. undaunted
    b. uncaring
    c. specific
    d. quiet

31.
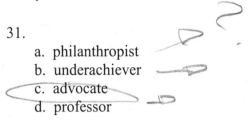
   a. philanthropist
   b. underachiever
   c. advocate
   d. professor

Select the answer that best completes the sentence or is closest in meaning to an underlined word.

"In respect of civil rights, common to all citizens, the Constitution of the United States does not, I think ___[32]___ any public authority to know the race of those entitled to be protected in the enjoyment of such rights....

It was said in argument that the statute of Louisiana does not discriminate against either race but prescribes a rule applicable alike to white and colored citizens...But this argument toes not meet the difficulty. Everyone knows that the statute in question had its origin in the purpose, not so much to exclude white persons from railroad cars occupied by blacks, as to exclude colored people from coaches occupied by or assigned to white persons. Railroad corporations of Louisiana did not make discrimination among whites in the matter of accommodation for travellers. The thing to accomplish was, under the guise of giving equal accommodations for whites and blacks, to compel the latter to keep to themselves while travelling in railroad passenger coaches. No one would be so wanting in candor as to assert the contrary. The fundamental objection, therefore, to the statute is that it interferes with the personal freedom of citizens....If a white man and a black man choose to occupy the same public ___[39]___ on a public highway, it is their right to do so, and no government, proceeding alone on grounds of race, can prevent it without infringing the personal liberty of each....

The white race deems itself to be the dominant race in this country. And so it is, in prestige, in achievements, in education, in wealth and power. . .But in view of the Constitution in the eye of the law, there is in this country no ___[42]___, dominant, ruling class of citizens. There is no caste here. Our Constitution is color-blind, and neither knows nor tolerates classes among ___[44]___. In respect of civil rights, all citizens are equal before the law. The humblest is the peer of the most powerful. The law regards man as man, and takes no account of his surroundings or of his color when his civil rights as guaranteed by the supreme law of the land are involved....

The arbitrary separation of citizens, on the basis of race, while they are on a public highway, is a badge of servitude wholly ___[48]___ with the civil freedom and the equality before the law established by the Constitution. It cannot be ___[49]___ upon any legal grounds...For the reasons stated, I am constrained to withhold my assent from the opinion and judgment of the majority."

-Dissenting Opinion of Justice John Marshall Harlan in the 1896 case of
Plessy v. Ferguson, 163 U.S. 537

32.
    a.   forbid
    b.   permit
    c.   disallow
    d.   reject

33. statute
    a.   law
    b.   state
    c.   statue
    d.   ruler

34. prescribes
    a.   medicates
    b.   imposes
    c.   rejects
    d.   pretends

35. guise
    a.   promise
    b.   prison
    c.   guide
    d.   pretense

36. wanting
    a.   lacking
    b.   full
    c.   used to
    d.   drifting

37. candor
    a.   dishonesty
    b.   straightforwardness
    c.   quiet
    d.   light

38. contrary
    a.   argument
    b.   hostility
    c.   opposite
    d.   manners

39.
    a. conviction
    b. corruption
    c. conscription
    d. conveyance

40. infringing
    a. arranging
    b. violating
    c. complimenting
    d. enjoying

41. deems
    a. designs
    b. considers
    c. rejects
    d. discriminates

42.
    a. inferior
    b. troubled
    c. fruitful
    d. superior

43. caste
    a. stone
    b. statue
    c. inherited social ranking system
    d. criminal

44.
    a. citizens
    b. schools
    c. universities
    d. trains

45. peer
    a. person equal in value to
    b. danger
    c. partner
    d. enemy

46. arbitrary
    a. televised
    b. random, authoritarian
    c. respectful
    d. restful

47. servitude

    a. honor
    b. convenience
    c. slavery
    d. service

48.
    a. consistent
    b. inconsistent
    c. justified
    d. in agreement

49.
    a. justified
    b. denied
    c. released
    d. resumed

50. assent
    a. opinion
    b. disagreement
    c. agreement
    d. satisfaction

Select the answer that gives the best synonym or definition.

51. prominent

    a. supportive
    b. well-known
    c. easily distracted
    d. obnoxious

52. testify

    a. to answer questions
    b. to place a telephone call
    c. to lie about
    d. to give evidence

53. negotiate

    a. to understand
    b. to discuss to reach an agreement
    c. to describe
    d. to restrict

54. acquiesce

    a. to submit or consent without objection
    b. to vehemently oppose
    c. to object on multiple grounds
    d. to strongly support

55. intensify

    a. to expose
    b. to expect improvement
    c. to strengthen or increase
    d. to weaken or decrease

56. compel

    a. to force
    b. to gain
    c. to lose
    d. to fight

57. allegiance

    a. greed
    b. friendship
    c. worship
    d. loyalty, faithfulness

58. eminent

    a. employable
    b. embarrassed
    c. experienced
    d. distinguished

59. monopolize

    a. to express
    b. to talk constantly
    c. to desire
    d. to control exclusively

60. annex

    a. to propose
    b. to add to a larger thing
    c. to attack
    d. to build higher

61. interdependence

    a. independent from another
    b. separation
    c. dependent on each other
    d. faithful loyalty

62. illusion

    a. false or misleading idea
    b. reference
    c. slight mention
    d. theater scene

63. prevalent

    a. advanced
    b. widespread or common
    c. unique
    d. dangerous

64. hostile

    a. informal
    b. formal
    c. unfriendly
    d. incurable

65. interval

    a. interest
    b. personal
    c. certainty
    d. time between

66. brevity

    a. shortness in time, speech, or writing
    b. pursuit of excellence
    c. intolerance
    d. worthless

67. ineligible

    a. important
    b. highly improved
    c. not qualified
    d. ungrateful

68. universal

    a. well-proven
    b. extremist
    c. existing everywhere
    d. sufficiently pleasing

69. fundamental

    a. purposeful
    b. basic or essential
    c. random
    d. frustrating

70. petition

    a. formal request for some privilege
    b. law
    c. specific right
    d. urgent message

71. deficient

    a. complete
    b. pure
    c. defensive
    d. incomplete or defective

72. vacillate

    a. articulate
    b. move
    c. fluctuate
    d. medicate

wavering, rising and going down.

73. obscure

    a. uncertain, ambiguous
    b. obvious
    c. easily understood
    d. straightforward

74. paradox

    a. box of treasures
    b. serious troubles
    c. seemingly contradictory
    d. distant lands

75. chronicle

    a. an advertisement
    b. a sequential record of events
    c. a serious illness
    d. ongoing

76. endeavor

    a. attempt, try
    b. understand
    c. finish
    d. experience

77. enterprise

    a. win a championship
    b. plan, venture
    c. enter without thinking
    d. principle

78. migrate

    a. fly away
    b. model
    c. early ambition
    d. move from one place to settle in another

79. deceptive

    a. false, fraudulent
    b. straightforward
    c. foolish
    d. desperate

80. procrastinate

    a. provide
    b. protect from harm
    c. delay, postpone
    d. privately agree

81. prudent

    a. wise, cautious
    b. primitive
    c. foolish, headstrong
    d. familiar with farming

82. diverse

    a. difficult, painful
    b. different, varied
    c. distant
    d. similar

83. concept

    a. idea, thought
    b. concrete, well established
    c. dance or festival
    d. fraction

84. endure

    a. ending
    b. quick effort
    c. fleeting
    d. last, persist

85. denounce

    a. stand for, mean
    b. speak against, publicly condemn
    c. strongly support
    d. destroy, discourage

86. requisite

    a. essential, needed
    b. unnecessary, unwarranted
    c. exquisite, expensive
    d. simple, plain

87. advocate

    a. adorn, wear proudly
    b. admonish, warn
    c. speak or write in favor of, publicly recommend
    d. demonstrate publicly

88. pardon

    a. burp loudly
    b. forgive, excuse
    c. promise in advance
    d. cut away a small part of

89. acclaim

    a. meekly accept
    b. announce ownership of land
    c. get accustomed to a new place
    d. praise, applaud

90. prohibit

    a. produce for inspection
    b. proceed without question
    c. be shy and quiet
    d. forbid, restrict

91. vengeance

    a. revenge, retribution
    b. mildly upset
    c. maddening situation
    d. hateful, poisonous

92. surpass

    a. surprise attack
    b. exceed, outdo
    c. bridge or river crossing
    d. overconfident

93. contemplate

    a. think, reflect
    b. construct, fabricate
    c. produce, manufacture
    d. accomplish at once

94. diminutive

    a. diminish, reduce
    b. divide into sections
    c. small, tiny
    d. disappear

95. discern

    a. destroy, pursue
    b. complete
    c. comprehend, understand
    d. confuse

96. consolidate

    a. unify, combine
    b. divide, destroy
    c. conquer
    d. put on the calendar

97. immense

    a. vast, enormous
    b. pleasure
    c. liquid
    d. measurable

98. ignorance

    a. belated
    b. lack of knowledge
    c. ignore a friend
    d. all-knowing, conceited

99. temperance

    a. moderation in action and speech, not drinking alcohol
    b. temperature outside
    c. understanding scientific principles
    d. simplification of goals

100. propaganda

    a. semblance of order
    b. recommendation of solutions to problems
    c. systematic efforts to spread beliefs or opinions
    d. rumor and gossip

101.   prohibit

    a. forbid under the law, prevent
    b. promise under law
    c. penalize, punish
    d. allow under the law

Select the answer that is closest in meaning to the underlined phrase.

102.   The services offered by the larger chain store couldn't hold a candle to those offered by the independent bookseller down the street.

    a. were not as bright as
    b. were physically inferior
    c. could not compare to
    d. were old-fashioned

103.   She blew hot and cold on whether to run for office this year.

    a. frequently changed her opinion
    b. penalized those who disagreed with her
    c. wondered what to do
    d. became alternately agitated and calm

104.   Even though they were twins, they would rarely see eye to eye about things.

    a. be the same height
    b. understand
    c. agree with each other
    d. confer or discuss with each other

105.   We knew who Joey would ask to the dance because he wore his heart on his sleeve.

    a. plainly showed his feelings
    b. had a broken heart
    c. felt everything very deeply
    d. drew a detailed picture

106. His father always told him that he should not make judgments about people until he had <u>walked a mile in their shoes</u>.
    a. borrowed their clothes
    b. stolen their shoes
    c. lived under similar circumstances
    d. hiked barefoot with others

107. From the look in Sam's eyes, I could tell he <u>got the picture</u>.

    a. took a photograph
    b. understood
    c. froze
    d. wondered what was happening

108. I left the party early because I had <u>other fish to fry</u>.

    a. to travel by boat
    b. to dive for fun
    c. other things to do
    d. cook dinner

109. When they arrive at their new destination, they may find out that they have <u>jumped from the frying pan into the fire</u>.

    a. gone from one problem to another
    b. fallen in love
    c. cooked dinner
    d. called the fire department for help

110. Their friendship was <u>as comfortable as an old shoe</u>.

    a. getting old and tired
    b. full of problems
    c. familiar and comfortable
    d. irregular and uncomfortable

111.   She knew she was <u>in hot water</u> when she forgot to go to the library after school to finish her homework.

   a.   sweating
   b.   in deep trouble
   c.   getting lucky
   d.   being a good friend

112.   She finished her research paper at <u>the eleventh hour</u> and barely managed to turn it in on time.

   a.   before midnight
   b.   after hours
   c.   at the latest possible moment
   d.   at the earliest convenience

113.   I planned to tell my grandma that I received an award, but my dad <u>stole my thunder</u>.

   a.   took it away
   b.   started to cry
   c.   heard a loud noise
   d.   did it first

In exercises 114 – 119, read the meaning, and then select the idiom from the choices.

114.   to use one's position to gain something

   a.   pull rank
   b.   pull up stakes
   c.   pull the plug
   d.   pull through

115.   something easily achieved

   a.   beat to the punch
   b.   piece of cake
   c.   see daylight
   d.   pull the rug out from under

116.   triumph

   a.   seize the day
   b.   make ends meed
   c.   let the cat out of the bag
   d.   carry the day

117.   visionary, unattainable scheme

    a. look out for
    b. as the crow flies
    c. castles in the air
    d. eat humble pie

118.   forced to choose between two unfavorable alternatives

    a. stuck between a rock and a hard place
    b. stuck up
    c. lay down the law
    d. gone to the dogs

119.   issue a challenge

    a. put up with
    b. throw down the gauntlet
    c. play fast and loose
    d. do the honors

Select the English meaning of the following foreign words or words derived from other cultures. Select the best meaning for any underlined word.

120.   The couple reviewed their finances and made a <u>bona fide</u> offer to purchase the house.

    a. unreasonable
    b. unexpected
    c. good faith
    d. insulting

121.   It would be a <u>faux pas</u> to discuss my affiliation with the President's opponents while I dined at the White House.

    a. frightening experience
    b. mistake
    c. rude gesture
    d. start of a war

122.   For the good of the students, the substitute teacher tried his best to maintain the <u>status quo</u>.

    a. time flies
    b. major changes
    c. the way things are
    d. differences of opinion

123. The protesters marched <u>en masse</u> to City Hall to confront the mayor.

    a. in a large group, all together
    b. loudly, aggressively
    c. one at a time
    d. ceremoniously, solemnly

124. carpe diem

    a. seize the day, make the most of the present
    b. nag, nag, nag
    c. a penny saved is a penny earned
    d. excuse me

125. caveat emptor

    a. the emperor is foolish
    b. an empty pot holds no water
    c. let the buyer beware
    d. cave dwellings with art

126. coup, or coup d'etat

    a. unsolved mystery
    b. embarrassing moment
    c. enclosure or high fence
    d. sudden, decisive political move, often effecting a change in government

127. circa

    a. about
    b. circus
    c. festival
    d. situation

128. My grandmother had a <u>penchant</u> for fine antiques and world travel.

    a. distaste
    b. aversion
    c. strong liking
    d. fear

129. My aunt's presentation of the triple-layered chocolate sponge cake was the _piece de resistance._

    a. most important or outstanding part
    b. fancy, pretentious, embarrassing
    c. forgotten, overlooked
    d. warlike, defiant

Select the answer that contains words with a common root.

130.
    a. vision, invincible
    b. visual, invisible
    c. vicious, vittles
    d. village, viable

131.
    a. compress, supression
    b. impress, involve
    c. increase, relocate
    d. pressure, force

132.
    a. convoluted, creation
    b. longitude, liberation
    c. centrality, eccentric
    d. symbolic, centrist

133.
    a. capitalize, congruent
    b. crude, croissant
    c. capitalize, decompose
    d. caption, capitalize

In the following exercises, identify the common prefix or suffix, and then select the choice that contains the correct meaning of that prefix or suffix in the given context.

134. circumstance, circulate, circumference, circumlocution, circular

   a. around
   b. under
   c. several
   d. over

135. bypass, bystander, byway

   a. extra
   b. not, never
   c. near, aside
   d. two

136. multitudes, multiply, multicultural, multicolored

   a. mixed
   b. many, much
   c. less
   d. back

137. abolish, abnormal, abstain, abhor, aberrant

   a. on
   b. near, beside
   c. from
   d. extra

138. interstate, intercede, interrupt, intervene, interpret, interchangeable

   a. few
   b. under
   c. among, between
   d. over

139. intrastate, intravenous, intramural, intracollegiate

   a. inside, within
   b. through
   c. among, between
   d. all

140. claustrophobic, triskaidekaphobia, agoraphobia, acrophobia, arachnophobia

    a. understanding
    b. wise
    c. state or quality
    d. fear of

141. thoughtless, careless, witless, ageless, tireless, childless

    a. like
    b. with
    c. without
    d. direction

Choose the best answer.

142. There is a strong _____ between the human heart and a mechanical pump.

    a. metaphor
    b. simile
    c. analogy
    d. imagery

143. After he crashed into the door, the bump on his head looked like a rhinoceros horn.

    a. This sentence contains no figurative language.
    b. This sentence contains a simile.
    c. This sentence contains a metaphor.
    d. This sentence contains an oxymoron.

144. After he crashed into the door, he applied a bag of ice to the throbbing rhinoceros horn above his eyebrows.

    a. This sentence contains no figurative language.
    b. This sentence contains a simile.
    c. This sentence contains a metaphor.
    d. This sentence contains an oxymoron.

145. Which of the following statements about the history of the English language is <u>not</u> true?

     a. Because it originated on an island, English changed little throughout the centuries and was not subject to outside influence.
     b. English changed substantially throughout the years because it originated on an island that suffered numerous foreign invasions throughout its early history.
     c. Latin influences in the English language are largely the result of when the Romans invaded England.
     d. The etymology of a word traces the origin and history of the word, as well as how its meaning and spelling have changed throughout the years.

146. The French influence on the English language

     a. began when the English invaded the French in 1066.
     b. transformed Old English into a new language known as Middle English.
     c. had little influence in the area of the language of government, law, and the military.
     d. has disappeared in Modern English such that few references from that period remain.

147. Which of the following statements about the historical influences on word meanings is <u>not</u> true?

     a. Many English words relating to architecture and painting originated in Italy, the birthplace of the Renaissance.
     b. Many English words relating to warfare and violence originated in Italian from the Roman influence.
     c. Scientific and technical words such as *diesel* and *Fahrenheit* come from the Chinese dynasties.
     d. French, Italian, Spanish, and Portuguese are referred to as Romance languages because they are based on Latin, the language spoken by ancient Romans.

148. Which of the following is <u>not</u> a way that new words generally come into our language?

     a. Dictionary editors create them in order to improve our language.
     b. We adopt them from other languages.
     c. We extend new meanings to words that already exist in our language.
     d. We combine existing forms of words to make new ones.

Content Cluster: READING COMPREHENSION OF
INFORMATIONAL MATERIALS

Objectives: To evaluate the student's understanding of: (1) the structural features of various informational materials, (2) the differences between original text and secondary sources, and (3) the elements of critical analysis of grade-level-appropriate text.

Parent Tip: It is fundamental that the skills tested in this content cluster improve with familiarity and practice. It is not surprising then, that the California Content Standard for Reading is that each student in grade 8 will read one million words annually on his own, from a variety of classic and contemporary literature, magazines, newspapers, and online information. The key to improving reading comprehension is to be an "active" reader who makes predictions and judgments about the material's content. Active readers of informational materials make it a practice to quickly scan a piece to note its component parts and look for subtitles that will give them clues about what they will read. They look at the pictures, charts, and graphs, too. They make mental or written notes about what they think they will read. Then, as they read the piece in its entirety, they monitor whether their predictions are confirmed or invalidated. They pause at various points in their reading to make sure they can restate in a simple way what they have read.

Select the best answer.

1. As a consumer it is important to understand the elements of

    a. contracts.
    b. warranties.
    c. instructional manuals.
    d. all of the above

2. In a written contract

    a. the terms are a good place to skim the document, especially if you have talked about them already with the other contracting party.
    b. it is essential to read the terms and conditions very carefully and to understand them completely.
    c. it is required that the final document be written by lawyers.
    d. the parties, signatories, witnesses, and guarantors are terms that mean the same thing.

3. A warranty

    a.   is a type of guarantee, commonly a promise by the seller that goods will be replaced or repaired if they are not as represented.

    b.   is rarely given in writing, particularly with respect to the sale of goods.

    c.   can be given under many circumstances, but is invalid if it promises that purchased goods are not defective.

    d.   usually does not recite the obligations of the seller or the buyer, or the time frame in which it is valid.

4. When analyzing expository writing, or writing that explains something,

    a.   it is important to focus on the persuasive elements of the piece.

    b.   it is important to identify the main idea and to look for clearly stated, specific facts that support the main idea

    c.   it is important to identify the theme, plot, characters, and setting.

    d.   it can be analyzed in precisely the same way that one analyzes narrative writing.

5. Which of the following would <u>not</u> be an effective logical order to use in a proposition-and-support pattern essay?

    a.   chronological order

    b.   spatial order

    c.   stream of consciousness

    d.   order of importance

6. A logical way to organize information about the provisions of the Articles of Confederation and the U.S. Constitution would be to

    a.   compare the two documents to focus on their similarities and contrast their differences.

    b.   focus on the lives of their authors of each document.

    c.   state the cause of the demise of the Articles of Confederation and the effects they had on foreign relations.

    d.   discuss them in order of importance to the nation.

Read the *Gettysburg Address* by Abraham Lincoln and the summary that follows. Refer to them for exercises 7 - 9.

"Four score and seven years ago, our fathers brought forth upon this continent a new nation, conceived in liberty, and dedicated to the proposition that all men are created equal.

Now we are engaged in a great civil war, testing whether that nation, or any nation so conceived and so dedicated, can long endure. We are met on a great battlefield of that war. We have come to dedicate a portion of that field as a final resting place for those who here gave their lives that this nation might live. It is altogether fitting and proper that we should do this.

But, in a larger sense, we cannot dedicate—we cannot consecrate—we cannot hallow—this ground. The brave men, living and dead, who struggled here, have consecrated it, far above our poor power to add or detract. The world will little note, nor long remember, what we say here, but it can never forget what they did here. It is for us, the living, rather, to be dedicated here to the unfinished work which they who fought here have thus far so nobly advanced. It is rather for us to be here dedicated to the great task remaining before us—that from these honored dead we take increased devotion to that cause for which they gave the last full measure of devotion; that we here highly resolve that these dead shall not have died in vain; that this nation,

under God, shall have a new birth of freedom; and that government of the people, by the people, for the people, shall not perish from this earth."

--Abraham Lincoln, November 19, 1863

Summary of the *Gettysburg Address*

Our nation was founded on the principles of freedom and liberty for all men. The soldiers who died in the Civil War to preserve our nation deserve to be honored, but we will never be able to honor them as much as they honored themselves by fighting so bravely for our nation and these principles. Now it is up to us, the living, to devote ourselves to the cause for which they died. Don't let them die in vain. Don't let our nation die, either.

7. The text of the Lincoln's speech is considered a(n)_____, while the summary is a _____.

    a.   oral source / written source
    b.   primary source / secondary source
    c.   secondary source / primary source
    d.   library source / natural source

8. The summary

    a. is too short to fulfill its purpose.
    b. should summarize each line of the original address.
    c. is adequate because it summarizes the main points of the speech.
    d. should be no more than one or two sentences long.

9. Depending upon the purpose of the summary,

    a. it might be helpful to quote a few of Lincoln's original words.
    b. it would be appropriate to have the summary be as long as the original speech.
    c. it would be appropriate to leave out crucial points for the sake of brevity.
    d. it would be appropriate to include details that are not relevant to the passage.

10. If you were moving to a new city, what sources would you consult to learn about the quality of the city's public schools?

    a. encyclopedias
    b. public library's map of the city
    c. statistics gathered by the State Department of Education
    d. *Who's Who* volumes

Read the following passage and answer questions 11 – 18.

The rotary haymaking machine is used for scattering and turning a mowed hay crop (grass, clover, legumes, etc.). First, the crop is cut close to the ground by a mower, which is either a tractor-drawn or a self-propelled machine whose cutting mechanism consists of a long flat cutter bar with forward-pointing slotted fingers and a <u>reciprocating</u> knife. As the crop is cut, it falls in a continuous <u>swath</u> on the ground, where it is left to <u>cure</u> until it is sufficiently dry to rake. Shortly after mowing, the <u>swath</u> is spread out so as to give maximum exposure to sun and wind and thereby promote drying. After a time, the spread hay has to be turned. The same machine can easily perform the spreading and turning operations.

Spreading (scattering) the freshly mowed swath is done by double-pronged raking forks mounted at the ends of arms which rotate about a vertical pivot. Each pivot carries four arms in a horizontal cross arrangement; these crosses operate in pairs, rotating in opposite directions. The whirling prongs rake the mowed grass together in front, and then fling it fanwise behind the machine over a relatively large width. Each rotating cross is supported on a wheel which follows all <u>irregularities</u> of the ground. The machine has an <u>articulated</u> frame, so that each cross can individually adapt itself to the <u>irregularities</u>. In another system there is a rigid frame, and every alternate wheel has a mounting which can telescope, thus permitting the wheel to move up or down. By means of a screw spindle, the rotary crosses can be varied in height in relation to the ground, so that the prongs can be set higher or lower. The arms are rotated at speeds of between 10 and 14 rpm. In this type of machine all the motions are <u>rotary</u>; there are no <u>reciprocating</u> parts. This operating principle makes for high efficiency. For instance, a machine with an operating width of 16 ft. (six "crosses" - i.e., sets of rotating arms) that is towed at a speed of 9-10 mph can deal with about 18 acres per hour.

Source: Complete Computer Solutions Website

11. reciprocating

    a. moving with an alternating backward and forward motion
    b. showing in return
    c. mutual
    d. reckless

12. swath

    a. sample of cloth
    b. body of water
    c. mowed row of grass, hay, or grain
    d. tractor

13. cure

    a. remedy for an illness
    b. treatment and healing
    c. to dry in order to keep
    d. antique

14. irregularities

    a. unruliness
    b. treatments and healing
    c. unevenness, not level or smooth
    d. rocks and stones

15. articulated

    a. jointed
    b. well-spoken
    c. expressive
    d. artistically painted

16. rotary

    a.   with a circular motion
    b.   slow
    c.   underground
    d.   inefficient

17. What would be the advantage of having the rotary crosses varied in height?

    a.   They maintain the integrity of the screw spindle.
    b.   They can cut crops that are different heights.
    c.   Most farmers are very tall.
    d.   There is no advantage.

18. A high performance rate is especially important

    a.   in climates where there are limited periods of favorable weather.
    b.   in climates where there are long periods of favorable weather.
    c.   if cost is not a factor in the decision to purchase or lease a machine.
    d.   if one is not concerned about efficiency.

Exercises 19 - 25 refer to the following passages:

An Environmental Impact Report (EIR) is the state equivalent of a federal Environment Impact Statement. The documents have a threefold purpose: (1) to analyze the environmental effects of a proposed project, (2) to identify ways to minimize or avoid any potential adverse effects that the project may have on the environment, and (3) to identify and assess alternatives to the proposed action.

*   *   *

DEPARTMENT OF THE INTERIOR
Bureau of Reclamation

Environmental Impact Statement/Environmental Impact Report on Sutter, Placer, El Dorado, Sacramento, and San Joaquin Counties, American River Water Resources Investigation

ACTION: Notice of intent to prepare an Environmental Impact Statement and Environmental Impact Report

SUMMARY: Pursuant to the National Environmental Policy Act of 1969, as amended, and the California Environmental Quality Act, the Bureau of Reclamation (Reclamation) and the Sacramento Metropolitan Water Authority (SMWA) propose to prepare a joint environmental impact statement/environmental impact report (EIS/EIR) on potential alternative solutions to meeting water-related needs in portions of all regions mentioned above, as identified through the American River Water Resources Investigation

(ARWRI). Reclamation and SMWA will propose possible alternatives representing themes ranging from demand management to all new construction.

MEETING DATE AND LOCATION: A public scoping meeting will be held Tuesday, April 11, 2000, 7:00 P.M., Stockton, California at the Stockton City Hall, 1 Center Drive.

FOR FURTHER INFORMATION CONTACT: Study Manager, Bureau of Reclamation, or Sacramento Metropolitan Water Authority. Letters of Inquiry may be sent to the address above.

SUPPLEMENTARY INFORMATION: The American River Water Resources Investigation began in 1992 and potential alternative solutions were developed. Three alternatives are being presented for further consideration: (1) conjunctive use (between ground water and surface water sources); conjunctive use with new storage (possible reservoir sites include Clay Station, Deer Creek, Duck Creek, and the possible enlargement of the existing Farmington Reservoir); and (3) the construction of a full-size Auburn Reservoir. The investigation is now at the point where the preparation of the EIS/EIR is ready to begin. Oral comments regarding the proposed alternatives are welcome at the public meetings. Written comments must be received at the above address by May 8, 2000, to ensure consideration in the development of the EIS/EIR.

19.   The document is a(n)

    a.   Notice of Intent to draft an EIS/EIR.
    b.   EIR
    c.   EIS
    d.   Joint EIS/EIR

20.   The Bureau of Reclamation

    a.   is part of the Department of the Interior.
    b.   is part of the SMWA.
    c.   does not deal with other federal departments or state agencies.
    d.   does not assist in the development of project alternatives.

21.   In the context of this document, reclamation is most likely

    a.   the reclaiming of coastal waters and public beach access.
    b.   the reclaiming of submerged land for cultivation or other use.
    c.   waste water.
    d.   products or uses of waste water.

22.   In the context of this document, the term *demand management* refers to

       a.   a public official's ability to manage complaints.
       b.   responses to newspaper letters to the editor.
       c.   decisions made regarding the regulation of water use.
       d.   land conservation strategies and the maintenance of open spaces.

23.   The reference to conjunctive use indicates

       a.   there may be a water shortage in the counties receiving the Notice.
       b.   there is an abundance of water in the counties receiving the Notice.
       c.   the investigation revealed fraudulent practices in Reclamation.
       d.   the construction projects in the counties will proceed immediately.

24.   The next step in the process is:

       a.   the SMWA will sue the counties listed in the Notice.
       b.   Reclamation and SMWA will prepare a joint EIS/EIR.
       c.   to construct reservoirs and additional water storage areas.
       d.   the American River Water Resources Investigation will begin immediately.

25.   The Stone family owns a ranch near the proposed site of the Auburn Reservoir. To
       learn more about the project they could

       a.   attend the meeting in Stockton or write a letter of inquiry to the Study Manager.
       b.   sue the Study Manager.
       c.   submit written comments to the Study Manager before May 8.
       d.   all of the above.

Exercises 26 - 35 refer to the following bylaws.

**LAKEVIEW HIGH SCHOOL
SCHOOL SITE COUNCIL BYLAWS**

Article I: Philosophy and Purposes

       The education of students requires the involvement and cooperation of the school,
home and community. The School Site Council ("SSC") shall provide a means for this
involvement and cooperation. The SSC will examine the programs and priorities of
Lakeview High School ("LHS") by assisting and advising the school staff in the
planning, implementation, modification, and evaluation of their instructional programs.
The SSC shall develop a school site plan, based on site needs, to continually improve the
LHS instructional program.

Article II: Membership

A.   Composition of the School Site Council

    1.   The voting members of the SSC shall be comprised of the following:

        a.   One-third of the voting members shall be comprised of LHS parents and/or community members (jointly, "parents" or "parent members"). LHS parents who are school employees may serve as voting members of the SSC.

        b.   One-third of the voting members shall be comprised of classroom teachers, the principal, and other interested staff members (jointly, "staff"). Classroom teachers shall comprise the majority of the staff members on the SSC.

        c.   One third of the voting members shall be comprised of LHS students, with at least one member representing each grade level in grades 8 through 12.

        d.   Only one person in a family shall serve as a voting member of the SSC.

    2.   Alternates shall have a voice in matters before the SSC, but no alternate shall be entitled to vote on the SSC, except in the event of an absence of a voting member.

B.   Selection and Election of School Site Council Parent Members

    1.   Interested persons may make application for service at any time by contacting the SSC Chairperson.

    2.   When the terms of voting members expire, candidates to replace parent voting members shall be randomly selected to stand for election to the SSC from among interested persons who have applied to serve on the SSC.

    3.   Alternates shall be selected in the following manner: After all candidates for parent voting members have been randomly selected, the remaining applicants may, if they choose, become candidates for parent alternates through a process of random selection, with the first name selected becoming the first alternate candidate, continuing seriatim.

    4.   All random selection shall take place in an open SSC meeting.

    5.   The names of the newly selected parent voting member candidates and alternate candidates shall be placed on a ballot, which shall be distributed to each family in the school.   The ballot shall allow the family to vote "in favor" of or "against" each candidate. A candidate shall become elected to the position for which he or she stood for election if he or she receives more "in favor" votes than "against" votes from among those valid ballots returned within the designated election period.

C. Terms of Office and Membership

1. Voting parent members will serve two-year terms. Each year, terms expire for one-half of the voting parent members, or the nearest approximation thereof. Voting staff members (except the principal) and student members will serve one-year terms.

2. No voting parent member may serve as such for more than two consecutive terms. No voting staff member (except the principal) may serve as such for more than four consecutive terms.

D. Voting Rights

1. A quorum shall consist of a simple majority of the voting membership.

2. Each voting member is entitled to one vote on matters that are placed before the SSC. A majority vote will carry, except when a two-thirds majority is required by these bylaws.

E. Special Committees

1. Special Committees shall have the authority to exercise the charges placed before them by the SSC. They may consist of SSC members and may include other persons from the school community who are not SSC members.

Article III: Meetings

A. Regular Meetings and Special Meetings

1. All meetings of the SSC shall be open to the public.

2. Special meetings may be called by the SSC Chairperson or upon the request of a majority of members of the SSC. Any special meeting shall have at least 24 hours notice.

Article IV: Bylaws

These bylaws may be amended at any meeting of the SSC by a two-thirds vote, provided that such amendments have been submitted to all SSC members not less than one week prior to the meeting at which the vote is to be taken.

26.   In addition to the LHS principal, there are four teachers, two staff members, and three students serving on the SSC. What additional voting members are required?

    a.   no additional members
    b.   two student members
    c.   four student members and two parent members
    d.   four student members and seven parent members

27.   Dr. Sanchez is an alternate member. If all of the voting members are in attendance at the SSC meeting, can Dr. Sanchez attend the meeting? If so, can he vote at the meeting?

    a.   no; no
    b.   no; yes
    c.   yes; yes
    d.   yes; no

28.   Mrs. Kramer, the parent of an LHS student in the twelfth grade, has been on the SSC since her son was in the eighth grade. This year

    a.   she can serve as a voting member.
    b.   she is not eligible to serve as a voting member.
    c.   neither she nor her son may serve on the SSC.
    d.   none of the above

29.   Ms. Montgomery, a security officer at the school, has a child who attends LHS. Ms. Montgomery

    a.   may serve as a voting member of the SSC.
    b.   is ineligible to serve as a voting member, but may be an alternate.
    c.   is ineligible to serve as a parent member because she is an employee of the school.
    d.   may serve on the SSC at the same time her child is a voting member.

30.   In order to become a voting member of the SSC,

    a.   one must first serve as an alternate.
    b.   one must be a parent, teacher, student, or principal of LHS.
    c.   one must be a community member, parent, LHS student, teacher, staff member, or principal.
    d.   one must be appointed by principal.

31.   How many regular meetings are required each year?

    a.   ten
    b.   twelve
    c.   six
    d.   none of the above

32.   Which of the following actions require a 2/3 vote?

    a.   a motion to approve the SI budget
    b.   a motion to change the bylaws.
    c.   a motion to approve a modification to the site plan
    d.   a motion to form a special committee to draft a homework policy

33.   Fourteen people are present at a regular meeting of the SSC. If the SSC is the
       minimum size set forth in the bylaws,

    a.   they may not conduct business.
    b.   they may conduct business.
    c.   they may discuss matters on the agenda, but their votes will not be binding.
    d.   they may conduct business once they have alternates for the absent members.

34.   Random selection would include

    a.   drawing names from a hat.
    b.   a group vote in any meeting
    c.   appointment by the SSC Chairperson
    d.   all of the above

35.   Officer Smith, from the Lakeview Police Department, is neither an SSC member,
       nor an LHS parent. Under the bylaws,

    a.   he is ineligible to serve on a special committee.
    b.   he must join the SSC in order to serve on a special committee.
    c.   he must be randomly selected and then stand for election.
    d.   he is eligible to serve on a special committee.

Exercises 36 - 39 refer to the following passage.

One of these sites began six years ago with two employees, yet now boasts more than 350 employees. Have you ever wanted to learn about how to invest in the stock market? Their guiding principle is that people should never invest until they understand what they are doing. That requires that people think, read, investigate, and research a particular company and an entire industry. There are some online sites that help non-professionals to understand about the stock market and investing money. Discussion boards are chronological permanent records of comments about a topic. Such sites are never successful sites.

36.   This paragraph is ineffective and confusing;

    a.   it lacks coherence because the thoughts skip around.
    b.   it is internally inconsistent and contains contradictions.
    c.   it lacks unity because it contains sentences that are not related to the main point.
    d.   all of the above

37.   To correct the internal inconsistency of this paragraph, the writer must

    a.   remove the first sentence only.
    b.   remove the second sentence only.
    c.   remove the sentence that mentions discussion boards.
    d.   remove the first and last sentences.

38.   To correct the lack of unity in this paragraph, the writer must

    a.   remove the sentence that mentions discussion boards.
    b.   remove the first sentence.
    c.   remove the last sentence.
    d.   all of the above

39.   If the writer rewrites the paragraph but does not delete any of the sentences, which sentence should come first?

    a.   There are some online sites that help non-professionals to understand about the stock market and investing money.
    b.   Have you ever wanted to learn about how to invest in the stock market?
    c.   Discussion boards are chronological permanent records of comments about a topic.
    d.   One of these sites began six years ago with two employees, yet now boasts more than 350 employees.

Content Cluster: LITERARY RESPONSE AND ANALYSIS

Objectives: To evaluate the student's understanding of: (1) the structural features of different forms of poetry; (2) the elements of plot, character, setting, and theme in literature; (3) significant literary devices that define a writer's style; and (4) how a work of literature reflects the author's culture and attitudes.

Parent Tip: Different types of writing require a different level of engagement on the part of the reader. Much of poetry and prose can be read for the sheer enjoyment of the experience. When analysis is required, however, encourage your child to make judgments about the veracity and plausibility of what is written. How are the attitudes and beliefs of the author reflected in the work? What would your child do if he or she were in the position of a particular character in literature? Examine the personalities and motivations of the characters, and analyze the effect that setting has on the plot. Discuss the theme that resonates in the work. Do the conflict and theme ring true? Is there a message that can be applied in everyday life?

Select the best answer.

1. Poetry

    a. is a kind of rhythmic writing.
    b. uses figurative language to try to appeal to the emotion and imagination of the reader.
    c. is a form of writing that may or may not rhyme.
    d. all of the above

2. A stanza is

    a. a random thought that does not fit into a theme.
    b. to a poem what a paragraph is to prose.
    c. a line in a rhyming poem.
    d. the attitude expressed by the poet.

3. The rhythm or pattern of accented and unaccented syllables in the lines of a poem is called

    a. end rhyme.
    b. free verse.
    c. meter.
    d. poetic beat.

In exercises 4 – 9, read the selection and select the best answer.

"But soft, what light through yonder window breaks?
It is the East, and Juliet is the sun.
Arise fair sun and kill the envious moon,
Who is already sick and pale with grief,
That thou her maid art far more fair than she."
 -William Shakespeare, *Romeo and Juliet*

4. This excerpt is an example of

 a. blank verse.
 b. free verse.
 c. rhyming iambic pentameter.
 d. a literary ballad.

5. This excerpt

 a. has no set meter, line, or rhyme pattern.
 b. is composed of unrhymed iambic pentameter.
 c. is an example of parallel poem.
 d. all of the above

6. Shakespeare uses this verse to describe

 a. the sunlight shining in the window.
 b. the stark contrast between sunrise and sunset.
 c. the sadness and loneliness of the night.
 d. Romeo's feelings about Juliet's beauty.

I Hear America Singing
Walt Whitman

I hear America singing, the varied carols I hear,
Those of mechanics, each one singing his as it should be, blithe and strong,
The carpenter singing his as he measures his plank or beam,
The mason singing his as he makes ready for work, or leaves off work,
The boatman singing what belongs to him in his boat, the deckhand singing on the
  steamboat deck,
The shoemaker singing as he sets on his bench, the hatter singing as he stands,

The woodcutter's song, the ploughboy's on his way in the morning, or at noon
  intermission, or at sundown,
The delicious singing of the mother, or of the young wife at work, or the girl singing
  or washing,

Each singing what belongs to him or her and to none else,
The day that belongs to the day—at night the party of young fellows, robust, friendly,
Singing with open mouths their strong, melodious songs.

7. This poetry is an example of

    a. blank verse.
    b. free verse.
    c. rhyming iambic pentameter.
    d. an elegy.

8. This poetry

    a. has no set meter, line, or rhyme pattern.
    b. lacks rhythm and balance.
    c. is composed of unrhymed iambic pentameter.
    d. is cinquain with pure meter.

9. Whitman's poem

    a. describes America's singing after the Civil War.
    b. explains the beauty of music in the world.
    c. encourages singing at work to increase productivity.
    d. celebrates the industriousness of Americans.

Exercises 10 - 17 either contain excerpts from different forms of traditional poetry, or describe a type of traditional poetry. In each exercise, read the poems and choose the best answer from the following choices:

    a. ballad
    b. lyric
    c. couplet
    d. epic
    e. elegy
    f. ode
    g. sonnet

10. "O Captain! my Captain! our fearful trip is done,
    The ship has weather'd every rack, the prize we sought is won,
        The port is near, the bells I hear, the people all exulting,
        While follow eyes the steady keel, the vessel grim an daring;
            But O heart! Heart! Heart!
             O the bleeding drops of red,
        Where on the deck my captain lies,
        Fallen cold and dead."
                --Walt Whitman,
                  from "O Captain! My Captain!"

11. "Did my heart love till now? Forswear it sight,
    For I ne'er saw true beauty till this night."
                --William Shakespeare,
                  from *Romeo and Juliet*

12. *The Odyssey* by Homer of Ancient Greece, which describes the adventures of the Greek hero Odysseus returning home from the Trojan War.

13. "When my love swears that she is made of truth
    I do believe her, though I know she lies,
    That she might think me some untutored youth,
    Unlearned in the world's false subtleties. . . ."
                --William Shakespeare

14. A poem that states the poet's personal feelings in fourteen lines, with ten syllables in each line and every other syllable is stressed, beginning with the second syllable

15. "Listen, my children, and you shall hear
    Of the midnight ride of Paul Revere,
    On the eighteenth of April, in Seventy-five;
    Hardly a man is now alive
    Who remembers that famous day and year. . . ."

    --Henry Wadsworth Longfellow,
    from "Paul Revere's Ride"

16. "Glad that I live am I;
    That the sky is blue;
    Glad for the country lanes,
    And the fall of dew. . . ."

    --Lizette Woodworth Reese,
    from "A Little Song of Life"

17. A long lyric, full of feeling and imagery

18. The elements of a story's plot line include

    a. the preface, beginning, middle, ending, and finale.
    b. the exposition, rising action, climax, falling action, and resolution.
    c. the setting, characters, theme, plot, dialogue, and point of view.
    d. the protagonist and the personality profile of the narrator.

19. With respect to conflict in a story's plot,

    a. external conflicts are rarely related to internal conflicts.
    b. it should generally be avoided so as not to unduly confuse the reader.
    c. it can not be between a person and him- or herself and still be considered true conflict.
    d. it can be any of the following types: person vs. person, person vs. society, person vs. him- or herself, person vs. nature, or person vs. fate.

20. Shakespeare's *Romeo and Juliet* and Laurents' *West Side Story*

    a. demonstrate that stories written three hundred years apart have little in common in terms of their setting, theme and conflict.
    b. are popular because their teenage characters face very little internal or external conflict in their daily lives.
    c. contain characters from different historical eras who confront similar external and internal conflicts.
    d. avoid the themes of thwarted love, parental control, and prejudice.

"I frequently tramped eight or ten miles through the deepest snow to keep an appointment with a beech tree, or a yellow birch, or an old acquaintance among the pines. I once had a sparrow alight upon my shoulder for a moment while I was hoeing in a village garden, and I felt that I was more distinguished by the circumstance than I should have been by an epaulet I could have worn." –*Walden, or Life In the Woods*, by Henry David Thoreau

21. Henry David Thoreau lived alone in the woods for two years. During this time he wrote Walden. This excerpt demonstrates that the tone of Thoreau's work was _____ toward nature.

    a. hostile
    b. reverent
    c. indifferent
    d. sarcastic

22. This excerpt is an example of

    a. the use of allegorical language.
    b. the use of figurative language.
    c. the effective use of similes.
    d. the use of understatement and irony.

23. As used by Thoreau, the word *distinguished* means

    a. being famous.
    b. feeling different from.
    c. appearing like an important person.
    d. perceptive.

24. An epaulet is

    a. an idea.
    b. a complex problem.
    c. a war hero's scar.
    d. an ornament worn on the shoulder.

Exercises 25 – 29 refer to the basic types of plot conflicts described below.

    a. an explorer faces a blizzard while climbing a mountain
    b. a new student stands up to the class bully
    c. an explorer questions his extreme fear of avalanches
    d. a girl overcomes poverty to be a corporate mogul
    e. a war veteran who loses his sight in battle must face life's new challenges

25. Which of the above situations is a person vs. person conflict?

26. Which of the above situations is a person vs. fate conflict?

27. Which of the above situations is a person vs. self conflict?

28. Which of the above situations is a person vs. nature conflict?

29. Which of the above situations is a person vs. society conflict?

30. Information about the setting of a novel or play can be found in

    a. the way the dialogue portrays dialects.
    b. descriptions of inventions and technology.
    c. references to attitudes and beliefs of the characters.
    d. all of the above

Exercises 31 - 38 refer to the underlined portions of the following excerpt of Chief Seattle's 1854 address to his people and a group of white settlers in the Pacific Northwest. Among the people in the audience was the governor of the territory, who had relayed to Chief Seattle President Pierce's proposal to buy Indian lands and move the Chief and his six tribes to a reservation.

"Yonder sky that has wept tears of compassion upon my people for centuries untold, and which to us appears changeless and eternal, may change. Today is fair. Tomorrow it may be overcast with clouds. My words are like the stars that never change. Whatever Seattle says the great chief at Washington can rely upon with as much certainty as he can upon the return of the sun or the seasons. The White Chief says that Big Chief at Washington sends us greetings of friendship and goodwill. This is kind of him for we know he has little need of our friendship in return. His people are many. They are like the grass that covers vast prairies. My people are few. They resemble the scattering trees of a storm-swept plain. . . .

It matters little where we pass the remnant of our days. They will not be many. The Indians' night promises to be dark. Not a single star of hope hovers above his horizon. Sad-voiced winds moan in the distance. Grim fate seems to be on the Red Man's trail, and wherever he goes he will hear the approaching footsteps of his fell destroyer and prepare stolidly to meet his doom, as does the wounded doe that hears the approaching footsteps of the hunter. . . .

We will ponder your proposition and when we decide we will let you know. But should we accept it, I here and now make this condition that we will not be denied the privilege . . . of visiting at any time the tombs of our ancestors, friends, and children. Every part of this soil is sacred in the estimation of my people. Every hillside, every valley, every plain and grove, has been hallowed by some sad or happy event in days long vanished. Even the rocks, which seem to be dumb and dead as they swelter in the sun along the silent shore, thrill with memories of stirring events connected with the lives of my people, and the very dust upon which you now stand responds more lovingly to their footsteps than to yours, because it is rich with the blood of our ancestors. . . ."

In each exercise, identify the literary device that Chief Seattle utilized in his speech. Select the most precise term that applies to the phrase or sentence. The choices are:

       a. simile
       b. metaphor
       c. analogy
       d. personification
       e. symbolism

31. Yonder sky that has wept tears of compassion

32. Today is fair. Tomorrow it may be overcast with clouds

33. My words are like the stars that never change.

34. Whatever Seattle says the great chief at Washington can rely upon with as much certainty as he can upon the return of the sun or the seasons.

35. They are like the grass that covers vast prairies.

36. They resemble the scattering trees of a storm-swept plain.

37. Wherever he goes he will hear the approaching footsteps of his fell destroyer and prepare stolidly to meet his doom, as does the wounded doe that hears the approaching footsteps of the hunter.

38. Which of Chief Seattle's words best reveal the Native American heritage and beliefs?

          a. Every part of this soil is sacred in the estimation of my people. Every hillside, every valley, every plain and grove, has been hallowed by some sad or happy event in days long vanished.
          b. The Indians' night promises to be dark.
          c. Sad-voiced winds moan in the distance.
          d. My people are few. They resemble the scattering trees of a storm-swept plain.

Content Cluster: WRITING STRATEGIES AND APPLICATIONS

Objectives: To evaluate the student's knowledge of: (1) how to write narrative, expository, persuasive, and descriptive texts; and (2) research, organizational, and drafting strategies.

Parent Tip: The California Standard is for eighth grade students to write narrative, expository, persuasive, and descriptive texts of 500 – 700 words. A good way to help them meet that standard is to show them examples of what they are trying to achieve. Have your child read many examples of high quality writing in each genre. Analyze the form of each selection, in effect, creating an outline that shows the structure or skeleton of the piece. Examine well-written paragraphs to see how the author makes her thoughts easy to follow. Finally, make sure your child expresses himself in writing every day in some way--in a journal, a poem, a cartoon strip, a plot outline for a short story; or a summary of a story heard on a news broadcast. Writing skills are improved like every other skill in life—through regular, informed, purposeful practice.

Exercises 1 and 2 refer to the following list of elements of paragraphs and essays.

    I.   a main idea expressed in a topic sentence
    II.   a main point presented in a thesis statement
    III.   a title
    IV.   an introduction
    V.   information that supports the main idea
    VI.   a body that presents supporting information
    VII.   a conclusion
    VIII. development of subtopics

1. A properly constructed paragraph contains which of these elements?

       a. II, III, VIII
       b. I, V
       c. II, IV, V
       d. II, III, IV, VI, VII, VIII

2. A properly constructed essay contains which of these elements?

       a. II, III, VIII
       b. I, V
       c. II, IV, V
       d. II, III, IV, VI, VII, VIII

3. A properly constructed thesis statement

    a. expresses a debatable point in an essay's introduction.
    b. expresses a statement of fact without any controversy.
    c. expresses a statement of the writer's personal belief system, as opposed to an opinion.
    d. all of the above

4. A properly constructed essay body

    a. is focused and states examples and explanations for every point.
    b. may be organized in a variety of logical ways, depending the complexity of the issue discussed.
    c. contains at least two paragraphs of information that specifically support the thesis
    d. all of the above

5. A properly constructed essay conclusion

    a. ends with a counterargument to the thesis.
    b. need not mention the thesis.
    c. ties the main points of the essay together.
    d. need not fulfill the reader's expectation as established by the thesis.

6. Which of the following statements would make an effective thesis?

    a. The sharecropping system that developed in the South after the Civil War was reminiscent of slavery, with economic bonds keeping blacks dependent on white farmers and merchants.
    b. It is unfair to judge Americans by examining their behavior in the five years that immediately preceded and followed the Civil War.
    c. The sharecropping system developed in America after the Civil War.
    d. President Johnson was impeached during Reconstruction

Exercises 7 - 9 refer to the following excerpt from a speech given by Susan B. Anthony in 1873.

"I stand before you under indictment for the alleged crime of having voted at the last presidential election, without having a lawful right to vote. It shall be my work this evening to prove to you that in thus doing, I not only committed no crime, but instead simply exercised my citizen's rights, guaranteed to me and all United States citizens by the National Constitution . . . [which] says:

We, the people of the United States, in order to form a more perfect union, establish justice, insure domestic tranquility provide for the common defense, promote the general welfare, and secure the blessings of liberty to ourselves and our posterity, do ordain and establish this Constitution for the Unites States of America.

It was we, the people, not we, the white male citizens, nor we, the male citizens; but we, the whole people, who formed this Union. We formed it not to give the blessings of liberty, but to secure them; not to the half of ourselves and the half of our posterity, but to the whole people—women as well as men. It is downright mockery to talk to women of their enjoyment of the blessings of liberty while they are denied the only means of securing them provided by this democratic-republican government—the ballot. . . ."

7. The first paragraph of the excerpt

     a. presents arguments in support of her position.
     b. clearly states the premise to be addressed in the next paragraph of the body.
     c. postpones stating its purpose, in an effort to obscure the main point.
     d. lacks a hook, unity, and coherence.

8. The last paragraph of the excerpt

     a. establishes unity and coherence by repeating key words.
     b. establishes unity and coherence by using parallel structures.
     c. lacks unity and coherence.
     d. both *a* and *b*

9. If one views the excerpt as a whole, Susan B. Anthony

     a. failed to support her thesis or conclusion.
     b. supported her thesis by quoting and paraphrasing the Constitution.
     c. failed to state a debatable point or stay on topic.
     d. supported her thesis by using a series of analogies to make her point.

10. When researching a significant historical issue, which of the following resources would be the <u>least</u> helpful?

    a. government documents
    b. books and encyclopedias
    c. primary sources such as diaries and letters
    d. observation and experiments

11. The texts of which of the following resources are generally <u>not</u> accessed through the internet?

    a. encyclopedias
    b. news articles
    c. books
    d. government documents

12. When researching a current political issue, which of the following resources generally would be the <u>least</u> helpful?

    a. encyclopedias
    b. interviews and opinion surveys
    c. newspaper and magazine articles
    d. newsgroups and listservs

13. When performing research on the internet,

    a. explore your topic using more than one search engine because each one is different.
    b. it is sufficient to use one search engine because they are all quite similar.
    c. there is no need to keep track of your searches.
    d. correct spelling of the keyword is not a factor because the search engine will identify misspelled words.

14. To use the internet to determine who first uttered the words "I will fight no more forever,"

    a. conduct an exact phrase search by printing the words in quotations.
    b. conduct an exact phrase search by selecting the "exact phrase" option on the search screen.
    c. would not be an effective way to find out this information..
    d. either *a* or *b*

15. When the results of your search have not hit an exact match of the information you are seeking,

    a. try the same search on another search engine.
    b. go to the closest match and select the "more like this" option.
    c. modify your search criteria and try again.
    d. all of the above

16. The _____ is responsible for evaluating the quality and credibility of a source on the internet.

    a. author of the published piece
    b. librarian
    c. reader
    d. internet search engine

In each of the following exercises, select the best revision of the sentence(s).

17. Everybody in my family likes music of some kind. In my opinion, jazz is the best. My brother likes hard rock music. My sister likes folk music. My mom and dad both like classical music alot. Then there's my other brother who like rock in addition to the other one. The fact of the matter is that basically we all love music.

    a. Everyone in my family love music. It's amazing to me that between two of us it's a tie for liking classical and rock. Jazz and folk are next.
    b. In my family of music lovers, my sister listens to folk music, my brothers like hard rock, my parents enjoy classical music, and I prefer jazz.
    c. There's musicians everywhere in my family—from liking jazz and folk, to my parents with choosing classical. In my opinion, jazz is better than rock, a point my brothers the rock fans disagree with.
    d. In my family of music lovers, my brothers like rock, my sister enjoys listening to folk artists, my parents are classical freaks, which leaves me for the jazz guru.

18. In my opinion, as I went through school, I learned the importance of getting myself organized, listening to every little thing that was said from the front of the room, to never procrastinate, last but not least, to have a good friend. I still believe and live by these practices.

    a. My opinion of how to get along in school is that it is important to get yourself organized, listen to everything said, to never procrastinate, and last but not least having a good friend is important. I still believe and live by these practices.

    b. In my opinion, as I went through school and afterwards into the present, I know that it is important to organize yourself, listen to everything, not procrastinating, and have a good friend to believe these practices.

    c. I learned many things in school, like getting myself organized, listen to everything the front of the room said, procrastinating is no good, but friends are. These things I still believe and live by.

    d. As a student I learned several important things that I still believe in and live by today: get organized, listen when others speak, never procrastinate, and always have a good friend.

19. New York City is a wonderful place. We go there all the time. You can go to the many wonderful restaurants to eat in and it is great to go to the theaters there. My favorite delicatessen has pictures of people who are famous who have eaten on the walls there. Though more than fifty years old, as you enter the main room a life-sized statue of Babe Ruth catches your attention.

    a. When visiting New York City I enjoy dining out and going to the theater. My favorite delicatessen in the city is more than fifty years old. Upon entering the place, several interesting items are noticeable. The entry contains a life-sized statue of Babe Ruth, and on the walls there are pictures of famous people who have eaten there.

    b. I enjoy taking my family for visits to New York, where we enjoy the tradition of eating in our favorite delicatessen before we enjoy going to the theater, too. It is enjoyable to look at the pictures of the people hanging on the wall who eat there. A fifty-year-old statue of Babe Ruth is as you enter to catch your attention.

    c. Because we go there all the time, New York City is a wonderful place. Even better is to eat at my favorite delicatessen for more than fifty years. Even if the food wasn't as good, you can still see Babe Ruth and the pictures hanging on the walls.

    d. No revision is necessary.

Select the best answer.

20. When writing a response to a piece of literature it is important to

    a. demonstrate that you have read the work carefully.
    b. discuss the writer's techniques and cite specific references to the text to support your claims.
    c. analyze elements such as theme, plot, character, and setting, and discuss how they affect the work.
    d. all of the above

21. In a narrative work, dialogue

    a. should reflect the way the characters would actually speak.
    b. should not have people interrupt each other or use bad grammar.
    c. should not be used to reveal a character's beliefs or problems.
    d. all of the above

22. Which of the following is <u>not</u> an appropriate element of a persuasive composition?

    a. stating your position clearly in favor of, or against, the proposition
    b. anticipating and addressing counter-arguments and reader concerns
    c. making personal attacks on the opponents
    d. supporting your position with well-organized and relevant information

23. Which of the following is <u>not</u> an appropriate salutation for a business letter?

    a. Dear Mrs. Cake:
    b. Gentlemen:
    c. Dear Sir,
    d. Dear Sir or Madam:

24. What is the proper sequence of the elements of a business letter?

    a. heading, salutation, body, signature
    b. heading, inside address, salutation, body, closing, signature
    c. date, heading, salutation, body , signature
    d. date, inside address, salutation, body, closing

25. Which of the following organizational styles is appropriate to use to write a technical document?

    a. process paragraph structured in chronological order
    b. narrative with comparison and contrast
    c. descriptive paragraph with sensory details
    d. classification paragraph with items grouped into categories for comparison

Content Cluster: SPELLING, GRAMMAR, PUNCTUATION, AND CAPITALIZATION

Objectives: To evaluate the student's: (1) spelling skills, (2) use of correct punctuation and capitalization, (3) use of correct grammar, and (4) skill in editing written work.

Parent Tip: Your child's mastery of the skills emphasized in this section will help him or her develop a clear, effective writing style. Once the content of a piece of writing is fully developed, a writer must pay close attention to the standard English conventions in order to turn a rough draft into a final, polished piece of writing.

Fill in the blank with the correctly spelled word.

1. For many years, our country _____ the _____ but equal doctrine.

    a. practiced / separate
    b. practist / separate
    c. practiced / seperate
    d. practised / separate

2. We _____ in the _____ of equal rights for all _____.

    a. belief / principle / people
    b. excell / principal / poeple
    c. exell / equality / people
    d. believe / principle / people

3. The _____ crops of the _____South were _____, cotton, and rice.

    a. principle/ antibellam/ tobacco
    b. principal / antebellem / tobbacco
    c. principal / antebellum / tobacco
    d. principle / antibellum/ tobbaco

4. Many early _____ in our nation were men of _____ and _____.

    a. polititions / wellth / privalige
    b. politicians / wealth / privilege
    c. politishans / welthe/ priviledge
    d. polititains / wealth / privalige

5. When writing _____ in a short story, it can be _____ for a _____
   to _____.

   a. dialoge / acceptable / character / exzagerate
   b. dialogue / acceptable / character / exaggerate
   c. dilogue / acceptible / charactor / exajerate
   d. diologue / exceptable / charicter / exagerate

6. I know _____ backpack this is, but _____ at the front door?

   a. whose / who's
   b. whos' / whose
   c. who's / whose
   d. whose' / whos'

7. It is _____ to close a _____ letter with "_____" or "Yours _____."

   a. appropreat / bisuness / Sinserely / truley
   b. apropreate / busness / Sincerely / truly
   c. appropriate / business / Sincerely / truly
   d. apropriate / busines / Sincerly, truly

8. After reading _____ the book, I had a _____ understanding of the _____.

   a. threw / thurough / thiery
   b. though / thorough / theory
   c. thought / through / theorry
   d. through / thorough / theory

9. _____ _____ the _____ child in the audience was _____.

   a. Every one / accept / mischevious / quite
   b. Everyone / ecxept / mischievious / quiet
   c. Everyone / except / mischievous / quiet
   d. Every one/ eccept / mischievous / quit

10. Her _____ _____ helped her to _____ _____ in high school.

   a. positive / attitude / achieve / success
   b. posative / attatude / acheive / sucsess
   c. positive / atitude / achieve / succes
   d. positiv / attitude / acheve / success

In exercises 11 - 35, identify the word that is spelled <u>incorrectly</u>.

	a.	b.	c.	d.
11.	definitly	definitely	answer	campaign
12.	concede	concsience	conscience	definitely
13.	conscious	analize	analyze	necessary
14.	boundries	annex	analysis	exceed
15.	compel	compelling	acknowlege	acknowledge
16.	courageous	category	believe	beleive
17.	acceptable	author	excede	enumerate
18.	persistant	successful	fulfill	receive
19.	desperately	destruction	distraction	destraction
20.	judgment	judgement	patient	permanent
21.	council	avoid	atached	daily
22.	dailey	counsel	organize	prevention
23.	worse	connect	organise	pencil
24.	influence	influince	collect	social
25.	available	avalable	traffic	expert
26.	indicate	settled	dangeruss	dangerous
27.	structire	structure	functional	instrument
28.	yesterday	factery	factory	fraction
29.	excellent	excerpt	extreme	exellent
30.	exerpt	elevator	embody	exemplary
31.	recommend	recomend	recognize	repeat

	a.	b.	c.	d.
32.	reduce	rhithim	terrible	trauma
33.	colledge	vegetable	education	enemy
34.	foren	audience	transportation	traffic
35.	forlorn	focus	sucsess	author

Identify the word that is spelled <u>correctly</u>.

36. environment	envirernment	enviernment	invierment
37. friten	frihten	frightten	frighten
38. curadge	curedge	couredge	courage
39. terible	terable	terrible	terrable
40. politicle	politicil	pollitical	political
41. cansle	cuple	cancel	cancle
42. firnichure	firnature	firniture	furniture
43. conect	connect	serius	cerious
44. dissatisfied	exausted	fasinating	focussed
45. tarriff	occurr	occurrance	occurrence
46. greatful	accomodate	embarrass	embarass
47. reinforce	resistence	relevent	recieve
48. prefered	irrelevant	irrelevent	ocuring
49. rithym	rhythym	rhythm	rythym
50. trajedy	trajidy	tradgedy	tragedy

	a.	b.	c.	d.
51.	noticeable	noticible	noticeible	unanymous
52.	persue	pursue	persew	pirsue
53.	wether	seige	siege	sutle
54.	persuasive	pursuasive	perserverence	sieze

In exercises 55 - 68, decide whether the text is without error, or whether it should be revised according to one of the choices.

55. My sister and I have an arrangement, she sets the table and I take out the trash.

   a. no errors
   b. I and my Sister have an arrangement. She sets the table and I take out the trash.
   c. My sister and I have an arrangement; she sets the table, and I take out the trash.
   d. My sister and I have an arrangement; She sets the table and I take out the trash;

56. Our teacher told us we were to noisy and so we quieted down imediately.

   a. no errors
   b. When our teacher told us we were to noisy, we quited down immediately.
   c. When our teacher told us we were too noisy, we quieted down immediately.
   d. Our teacher told us we were too noisy, because we quieted down immediately.

57. I enjoyed watching the speech. Mostly it was funny. And always interesting; although sad in parts.

   a. no errors
   b. Although the speech was sad sometimes it was interesting, and I liked it because it was mostly funny.
   c. The speech: I liked it, because it was always sad and funny and interesting.
   d. Although the speech was sad in parts, I liked it because it was mostly funny and always interesting.

58. Did the Principal say who would be talking to we girls about the problem.

   a. no errors
   b. Did the principal say who would be talking to us girls about the problem?
   c. Did the Principle say who would be talking to us girls about the problem?
   d. Did the principal say whom would be talking to we girls about the problem?

59. Did your father say to whom we would be speaking at the airport?

    a. No errors
    b. Did your Father say to whom we would be speaking at the Airport?
    c. Did your father say to who we would be speaking at the Airport?
    d. Did your father say who we would be speaking to at the Airport?

60. As Martin Luther King stated in his "I Have a Dream" speech, "[A]s we walk, we must make the pledge that we shall always march ahead. We cannot turn back."

    a. No errors
    b. As Martin Luther King stated in his I Have a Dream speech "as we walk, we must make the pledge that we shall always march ahead. We cannot turn back."
    c. As Martin Luther King stated in his "I Have a Dream speech, "(A)s we walk, we must make the pledge that we shall always march ahead. We cannot turn back."
    d. As Martin Luther King stated in his I Have a Dream speech; As we walk, we must make the pledge that we shall always march ahead. We cannot turn back.

61. Asian fusion cuisine is a combination of pacific rim recipes and french food.

    a. No errors
    b. Asian Fusion Cuisine is a combination of: Pacific Rim Recipes and French Food.
    c. Asian fusion cuisine is a combination of Pacific Rim recipes and French food.
    d. Asian fusion Cuisine is a combination of Pacific Rim Recipes and French Food.

62. My history teachers' eyes filled with tears when she spoke of president Kennedys legacy to the nation.

    a. No errors
    b. My History Teacher's eyes filled with tears when she spoke of President Kennedys' legacy to the nation.
    c. My history teachers' eyes filled with tears when she spoke of President Kennedy's legacy to the Nation.7
    d. My history teacher's eyes filled with tears when she spoke of President Kennedy's legacy to the nation.

63. The onlookers cheered for the champions and congratulated the runner-ups too.

   a. No errors
   b. The onslooker cheered for the champions and congratulated the runner-ups too.
   c. The onslookers cheered for the champions and congratulated the runners-ups too.
   d. The onlookers cheered for the champions and congratulated the runners-up, too.

64. California is a wonderful place to visit because people can walk among the redwoods the tallest trees in the world and the sequoia trees the largest living things in the world.

   a. No errors
   b. California is a wonderful place to visit. Because people can walk among the redwoods, the tallest trees in the world and the sequoia trees the largest living things in the world.
   c. California is a a wonderful place to visit. People can walk among the redwoods (the tallest trees in the world) and the sequoia trees (the largest living things in the world).
   d. California is a a wonderful place to visit; Because people can walk among the redwoods, the tallest trees in the world, and the sequoia trees, the largest living things in the world.

65. Rugby is a kicking, passing, and tackling game that originated in England and is the direct ancestor of american football, and the game is popular in Great Britain, Reance, australia, New Zealand, and South Africa, it is also played in many other places.

   a. No errors
   b. Rugby is a kicking, passing, and tackling game that originated in England and is the direct ancestor of american football, and the game is popular in Great Britain, Reance, australia, New Zealand, and South Africa; it is also played in many other places.
   c. Rugby is a kicking, passing, and tackling game that originated in England. It is the direct ancestor of american football, and the game is popular in Great Britain, France, Australia, New Zealand, and South Africa, it is also played in many other places.
   d. Rugby is a kicking, passing, and tackling game that originated in England. It is the direct ancestor of American football. The game is popular in Great Britain, France, Australia, New Zealand, and South Africa, although it is played in many other places.

66. My Grandfather is fluent in Spanish because this is the language you learn when you grow up in Mexico.

    a.　No errors
    b.　My grandfather is fluent in spanish because this is the language you learn when you grow up in Mexico.
    c.　My grandfather is fluent in Spanish because this is the language you learned when you grew up in Mexico.
    d.　My grandfather is fluent in Spanish because this is the language he learned when he grew up in Mexico.

67. Either Samantha or Maria will ask their parents to drive all of us to the basketball game.

    a.　No errors
    b.　Either Samantha or Maria will ask their parents to drive them to the basketball game.
    c.　Either Samantha or Maria will ask her parents to drive all of us to the basketball game.
    d.　Either Samantha, or Maria, will ask their parents whether or not they can drive them to the basketball game.

68. I have attended both Jefferson School and Washington School, but I like Jefferson best. Even though I have to except the fact that it's football team does worst between the two of them.

    a.　No errors
    b.　I have attended Jefferson School and Washington School. Between the two, I like Jefferson better, even though its football team is worse.
    c.　I have attended Jefferson and Washington Schools, and between the two of them, I like Jefferson better, even though its football team is worser.
    d.　I have attended Jefferson School and Washington School. I like Jefferson the best of the two of them, because their football team is the best.

Exercises 69 - 73 refer to the following passage. In each exercise, decide whether the text should be revised according to one of the choices.

[*1*] Her royal subjects call her the Queen Mum. [*2*] She is beloved. [*3*] British television covered her live for her 100th birthday celebration. [*4*] She came out to greet the at least 40,000 of loyal subjects who cheered for her out on the balcony at Buckingham Palace. [*5*] She addressed the people of Great Britain. [*6*] Many of them haven't heard her voice ever before. [*7*] She has not granted an interview in 77 years. [*8*] Authors scrounge anything in print about her to have something to quote. [*9*] She was born Elizabeth Bowes-Lyon in 1900 on August 4. [*10*] Queen Victoria was queen then. William McKinley was the U.S. President then. [*11*] Marconi invented the wireless radio in 1896, women are participating in the Olympics for the first time in Paris in 1900, and Orville and Wilber Wright fly the first successful airplane in 1903. [*12*] In 1905 Albert Einstein announces his theory of relativity of time and space ($E=mc^2$). [*13*] She sort of became queen by accident because she married Prince Albert who was the younger brother of Edward VIII who was the heir to the throne. [*14*] Then he abdicated the throne to marry an American. [*15*] Her name was Wallace Simpson. [*16*] It was quite a scandal! [*17*] That means he becomes King George VI in 1936 and she is now Queen Elizabeth. [*18*] She helped her people make it through World War II.. [*19*] He died in 1952. [*20*] Their daughter who is also Elizabeth becomes the new Queen. [*21*] Her mother is now the Queen Mother. [*22*] Diana, the Princess, is no longer living, however.

69. [*1*] Her loyal subjects call her the Queen Mum. [*2*] She is beloved. [*3*] British television covered her live for her 100th birthday celebration. [*4*] She came out to greet the at least 40,000 of loyal subjects who cheered for her out on the balcony at Buckingham Palace.

   a. No revisions
   b. Last week, more than 40,000 loyal subjects cheered wildly as their beloved Queen Mum emerged from Buckingham Palace to wave to them from the balcony on the occasion of her 100th birthday. British television provided live coverage of the event.
   c. 40,000 people in one place is a lot of people, even if it is to come to see the queen's mother for her 100th birthday. Even the television covered her.
   d. Last week 40,000 people came to the balcony of Buckingham Palace to see the Queen Mum turn 100 years old on her birthday in England.

70. [5] She addressed the people of Great Britain. [6] Many of them haven't heard her voice ever before. [7] She has not granted an interview in 77 years. [8] Authors scrounge anything in print about her to have something to quote from her.

    a. No revisions
    b. She has not granted an interview in 77 years. Authors scrounge anything in print about her to have something to quote from her. So she talked to the people of Great Britain.
    c. She addressed the people of Great Britain which was a treat for them. Before that many of them haven't heard her voice ever before because she has not granted an interview in 77 years. Authors scrounge anything in print about her to have something to quote from her.
    d. Although it was *her* birthday, she gave her subjects a present by addressing them via television. Many of them had never heard her voice before, as she had not granted an interview in 77 years.

71. [9] She was born Elizabeth Bowes-Lyon in 1900 on August 4. [10] Queen Victoria was queen then. William McKinley was the U.S. President then. [11] Marconi invented the wireless radio in 1896, women are participating in the Olympics for the first time in Paris in 1900, and Orville and Wilber Wright fly the first successful airplane in 1903. [12] In 1905 Albert Einstein announces his theory of relativity of time and space ($E=mc^2$).

    a. When she was born Elizabeth Bowes Lyon on August 4, 1900, women are participating in the Olympics for the first time. The Wright Brothers are in the future and Albert Einstein almost, also.
    b. She was born before the Wright Brothers and Albert Einstein, when women could be in the Olympics.
    c. The world has changed since her birth in 1900 when Queen Victoria ruled England, William McKinley was President of the United States, and the Wright Brothers had not yet flown their airplane. It would be another five years before Albert Einstein announced his theory of relativity, $E=mc^2$.
    d. In 1900 when she was born Albert Einstein, he had not even announced his theory of relativity, however Marconi had already invented the wireless radio.

72. [*13*] She sort of became queen by accident because she married Prince Albert who was the younger brother of Edward VIII who was the heir to the throne. [*14*] Then he abdicated the throne to marry an American. [*15*] Her name was Wallace Simpson. [*16*] It was quite a scandal! [*17*] That means he becomes King George VI in 1936 and she is now Queen Elizabeth. [*18*] She helped her people make it through World War II.. [*19*] He died in 1952. [*20*] Their daughter who is also Elizabeth becomes the new Queen. [*21*]Her mother is now the Queen Mother.

   a. She became a queen in 1936, when her husband became a king. He died in 1952 when her daughter inherited the throne and she became the Queen Mother.
   b. She married Prince Albert, the younger brother of the heir to the throne, Edward VIII. But when Edward abdicated in 1936, Albert was crowned King George VI, and Elizabeth became Queen. Upon his death in 1952, their daughter inherited the throne, and her mother became the Queen Mother.
   c. By accident she married someone who eventually became king. Then their daughter became queen and her mother was called the Queen Mum.
   d. She helped her people make it through World War II.. He died in 1952.and their daughter who is also Elizabeth becomes the new Queen. Her mother now became the Queen Mother.

73. In a revision of the passage,

   a. there should be at least two paragraphs, perhaps three.
   b. every sentence from the original should be included because each one is relevant to the topic.
   c. the sentence structure in the original should be maintained, but the order of the sentences could be changed.
   d. all of the above

74. To improve the unity of the passage, the writer should

   a. fix the contradictions in sentences 9 – 13.
   b. fix the contradictions in sentences 2 and 18.
   c. delete sentence 22.
   d. delete sentences 13 and 14.

75. In subsequent revisions of the passage, the writer should

   a. make the verb tenses more consistent.
   b. join some of the simple sentences and develop some complex sentences.
   c. make the writing more precise and delete the irrelevant sentences.
   d. all of the above.

LANGUAGE ARTS
ANSWER KEY

Word Analysis
1. b
2. b
3. c
4. a
5. a
6. d
7. c
8. c
9. d
10. a
11. b
12. c
13. d
14. c
15. a
16. d
17. c
18. b
19. a
20. a
21. d
22. b
23. c
24. a
25. b
26. a
27. c
28. b
29. b
30. a
31. c
32. b
33. a
34. b
35. d
36. a
37. b
38. c
39. d
40. b
41. b

42. d
43. c
44. a
45. a
46. b
47. c
48. b
49. a
50. c
51. b
52. d
53. b
54. a
55. c
56. a
57. d
58. d
59. d
60. b
61. c
62. a
63. b
64. c
65. d
66. a
67. c
68. c
69. b
70. a
71. d
72. c
73. a
74. c
75. b
76. a
77. b
78. d
79. a
80. c
81. a
82. b
83. a

84. d
85. b
86. a
87. c
88. b
89. d
90. d
91. a
92. b
93. a
94. c
95. c
96. a
97. a
98. b
99. a
100. c
101. a
102. c
103. a
104. c
105. a
106. c
107. b
108. c
109. a
110. c
111. b
112. c
113. d
114. a
115. b
116. d
117. c
118. a
119. b
120. c
121. b
122. c
123. a
124. a
125. c

126. d
127. a
128. c
129. a
130. b
131. a
132. c
133. d
134. a
135. c
136. b
137. c
138. c
139. a
140. d
141. c
142. c
143. b
144. c
145. a
146. b
147. c
148. a

Reading Comprehension
1. d
2. b
3. a
4. b
5. c
6. a
7. b
8. c
9. a
10. c
11. a
12. c
13. c
14. c
15. a
16. a

17. b
18. a
19. a
20. a
21. b
22. c
23. a
24. b
25. a
26. d
27. d
28. b
29. a
30. c
31. d
32. b
33. b
34. a
35. d
36. d
37. d
38. d
39. b

Literary Response & Analysis
1. d
2. b
3. c
4. a
5. b
6. d
7. b
8. a
9. d
10. e
11. c
12. d
13. g
14. g
15. a
16. b
17. f
18. b
19. d
20. c

21. b
22. b
23. c
24. d
25. b
26. e
27. c
28. a
29. d
30. d
31. b or d
32. e
33. a
34. c
35. a
36. a
37. c
38. a

Writing Strategies & Applications
1. b
2. d
3. a
4. d
5. c
6. a
7. b
8. d
9. b
10. d
11. c
12. a
13. a
14. d
15. d
16. c
17. b
18. d
19. a
20. d
21. a
22. c
23. c
24. b
25. a

Conventions
1. a
2. d
3. c
4. b
5. b
6. a
7. c
8. d
9. c
10. a
11. a
12. b
13. b
14. a
15. c
16. d
17. c
18. a
19. d
20. b
21. c
22. a
23. c
24. b
25. b
26. c
27. a
28. b
29. d
30. a
31. b
32. b
33. a
34. a
35. c
36. a
37. d
38. d
39. c
40. d
41. c
42. d
43. b
44. a
45. d

46. c
47. a
48. b
49. c
50. d
51. a
52. b
53. c
54. a
55. c
56. c
57. d
58. b
59. a
60. a
61. c
62. d
63. d
64. c
65. d
66. d
67. c
68. b
69. b
70. d
71. c
72. b
73. a
74. c
75. d

MATH

Content Cluster: ALGEBRA – Section 1

Objective: Students will identify and use the arithmetic properties of integers, rational, irrational, and real numbers.

Parent tip: Math is like a foreign language. It is very important for the student to become familiar with the vocabulary. In most algebra books, the properties are listed in a summary in the early chapters. Teachers will use the vocabulary when instructing students. Flash cards can be helpful for students to understand the properties.

Directions: Choose the correct answer. Use the right side of the page to write out the problems.

1. $3(x-y) = 3x - 3y$ illustrates what property?

   a. Identity Property
   b. Associative Property
   c. Commutative Property
   d. Distributive Property

2. $3x + 4y = 4y + 3x$ illustrates what property?

   a. Identity Property
   b. Associative Property
   c. Commutative Property
   d. Distributive Property

3. $4x + 0 = 4x$ illustrates what property?

   a. Identity Property
   b. Associative Property
   c. Commutative Property
   d. Distributive Property

4. $1x = x$ illustrates what property?

   a. Identity Property
   b. Associative Property
   c. Commutative Property
   d. Distributive Property

5. Which answer illustrates the additive inverse property?

    a. $4 \cdot \dfrac{1}{4} = 1$

    b. $6 + 3 = 3 + 6$

    c. $-4 + 4 = 0$

    d. $5 + 0 = 5$

6. Which answer illustrates the associative property for addition?

    a. $2 (3x) = (2 \cdot 3) x$

    b. $6 (x + y) = 6x + 6y$

    c. $(-3x) + 3x = 0$

    d. $4 + (5 + x) = (4 + 5) + x$

7. Which answer illustrates the commutative property for multiplication?

    a. $4 (x + y) = 4x + 4y$

    b. $4 (x + y) = (x + y) 4$

    c. $4 (x + y) = 4 (y + x)$

    d. $4 (x + y) = 4 (x + y)$

8. Which one of the following is **not** an example of the identity property for multiplication or addition?

    a. $3 \cdot \dfrac{1}{3} = 1$

    b. $3 + 0 = 3$

    c. $3 \cdot 1 = 3$

    d. $1 \cdot 0 = 0$

9. Which one of the following is **not** an example of the closure property?

    a. $6 \div 0$ is a real number

    b. $5 \cdot 3$ is a real number

    c. $7 - 0$ is a real number

    d. $8 + {-}2$ is a real number

10. Which one of the following is **not** an example of the commutative properties for addition or multiplication?

    a. $3 + 8 = 8 + 3$

    b. $abc = acb$

    c. $2 (x + y) = 2 (y + x)$

    d. $7xy = 7xy$

Content Cluster: ALGEBRA - Section 2

Objective: Students will understand the use of operations such as taking the opposite, reciprocal, raising to a power, and taking a root. This includes the rules for exponents.

> **Parent Tip:** Once again, vocabulary is a key to understanding algebra. The opposite of 3 is –3, or in symbols, the opposite of x is –x. The reciprocal of 3 is $\frac{1}{3}$, or in symbols, the reciprocal of x is $\frac{1}{x}$ if $x \neq 0$. The number 2 can be raised to a power 3 by writing it as 2^3. 2 is the base, where 3 is the exponent ($2^3 = 2 \cdot 2 \cdot 2$). The square root of 9 ($\sqrt{9}$) is 3, since $3 \cdot 3$ or $3^2 = 9$.

Directions: Choose the correct answer.

1. Find the opposite of $-\frac{2}{3}$.

   a. $-\frac{3}{2}$
   b. $\frac{2}{3}$
   c. $-\frac{2}{3}$
   d. $\frac{3}{2}$

2. Find the reciprocal of $-\frac{2}{3}$.

   a. $-\frac{3}{2}$
   b. $\frac{2}{3}$
   c. $-\frac{2}{3}$
   d. $\frac{3}{2}$

3. 3^4 is equivalent to _____.

   a. $4 \cdot 4 \cdot 4$
   b. $3 \cdot 3 \cdot 3 \cdot 3$
   c. 12
   d. $4 \cdot 4 \cdot 4 \cdot 4$

4. The square root of 36 is written as

   a. $3 + 6$
   b. 6^2
   c. 36^2
   d. $\sqrt{36}$

5. To solve the equation 2x + 5 = 9, the first step is to

    a. add –5 to both sides.
    b. add –9 to both sides.
    c. multiply by 2 to both sides.
    d. add –2 to both sides.

6. To solve the equation $-\dfrac{3}{4}x = 12$, you should

    a. multiply by $\dfrac{3}{4}$ to both sides.

    b. multiply by $\dfrac{4}{3}$ to both sides.

    c. multiply by $-\dfrac{4}{3}$ to both sides.

    d. multiply by $-\dfrac{3}{4}$ to both sides.

7. To solve the equation $\sqrt{x} = 5$, you should

    a. square root both sides.
    b. square both sides.
    c. add –5 to both sides.
    d. add 5 to both sides.

8. To solve the equation $x^2 = 36$, you should

    a. square root both sides.
    b. square both sides.
    c. add 36 to both sides.
    d. add –36 to both sides.

Parent Tip: Flash cards can be helpful to learn the rules for exponents.
$x^a \cdot x^b \cdot x^{a+b}$, $\dfrac{x^a}{x^b} = x^{a-b}$ if a>b, $\dfrac{x^a}{x^b} = \dfrac{1}{x^{b-a}}$ if b>a (Remember the bases of the exponent must be the same. $(x^a)^b = x^{ab}$.

EXAMPLES: $2^3 \cdot 2^7 = 2^{10}$, $\dfrac{2^8}{2^3} = 2^5$, $\dfrac{2^3}{2^7} = \dfrac{1}{2^4}$, $(2^4)^5 = 2^{20}$.

Simplify questions 9 – 16.

9. $3^4 \cdot 3^5$

    a. 3^{20}
    b. 6^9
    c. 3^9
    d. 6^{20}

10. $(3^2)^4$

    a. 3^6
    b. 3^{16}
    c. 3^{12}
    d. 3^8

11. $x^4 \cdot x^6 \cdot x^5$

    a. x^{15}
    b. $3x^{15}$
    c. $3x^5$
    d. x^{120}

12. $\dfrac{3^{12}}{3^4}$

    a. 3^3
    b. 3^8
    c. 1^8
    d. 1^3

13. $\dfrac{x^6}{x^{12}}$

    a. x^2
    b. $\dfrac{1}{2}$
    c. $\dfrac{1}{x^6}$
    d. $\dfrac{1}{x^2}$

14. $(x^3)^4$

    a. x^7
    b. x^{81}
    c. x^{12}
    d. $4x^3$

15. $(2x^3)(3x^4)$

    a. $6x^7$
    b. $5x^7$
    c. $6x^{12}$
    d. $5x^{12}$

16. $\dfrac{12x^8}{16x^4}$

    a. $\dfrac{3x^2}{4}$
    b. $\dfrac{3x^4}{4}$
    c. $\dfrac{x^4}{4}$
    d. $\dfrac{x^2}{4}$

Parent Tip: Negative exponents can quickly be changed into positive exponents with the following rules. $x^{-a} = \dfrac{1}{x^a}$ and $\dfrac{1}{x^{-a}} = x^a$

Simplify the following.

17. $\dfrac{x^{-5}}{x^3}$

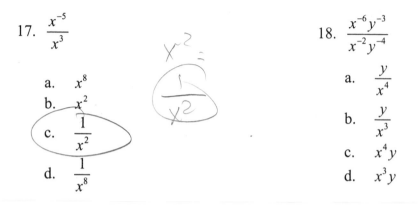

    a. x^8

    b. x^2

    c. $\dfrac{1}{x^2}$

    d. $\dfrac{1}{x^8}$

18. $\dfrac{x^{-6}y^{-3}}{x^{-2}y^{-4}}$

    a. $\dfrac{y}{x^4}$

    b. $\dfrac{y}{x^3}$

    c. $x^4 y$

    d. $x^3 y$

19. $(x+y)^{-1}$

    a. $x+y$

    b. $\dfrac{1}{x} + \dfrac{1}{y}$

    c. $\dfrac{1}{x+y}$

    d. $-x-y$

20. $\dfrac{-6x^{-2}}{2x}$

    a. $\dfrac{1}{3x^3}$

    b. $\dfrac{-3}{x^3}$

    c. $\dfrac{-1}{3x^3}$

    d. $-3x^3$

Content Cluster: ALGEBRA - Section 3

Objective: Students will solve equations and inequalities involving absolute values.

Parent Tip: Separating the absolute equation or inequality into 2 parts can solve absolute value equations and inequalities.

$\quad$ **EXAMPLES:** $\quad |x| = 5$ will separate into $x = 5$ or $x = -5$.

$\qquad\qquad\qquad\quad |x| > 4$ will separate into $x > 4$ or $x < -4$.

$\qquad\qquad\qquad\quad |x| < 3$ will separate into $x < 3$ and $x > -3$ or $-3 < x < 3$.

Remember to solve for the absolute value before separation.

$\quad$ **EXAMPLE:** $\quad |3x + 1| - 2 > 5$ must be transformed to $|3x+1| > 7$ before separation.

Solve the following equations and inequalities.

1. $|2x + 3| \geq 7$ is equivalent to

   a. $2x + 3 \geq 7$ and $2x + 3 \leq -7$
   b. $2x + 3 \geq 7$ or $2x + 3 \leq 7$
   c. $2x + 3 \geq 7$ or $2x + 3 \leq -7$
   d. $2x + 3 \leq 7$ or $2x + 3 \leq -7$

2. $|x - 3| \leq 6$ is equivalent to

   a. $x - 3 \leq 6$ and $x - 3 \geq 6$
   b. $x - 3 \leq 6$ and $x - 3 \geq -6$
   c. $x - 3 \leq -6$ and $x - 3 \geq -6$
   d. $x - 3 \leq 6$ or $x - 3 \geq -6$

3. $-5 < 2x - 1 < 5$ is equivalent to

   a. $|2x - 1| < 5$
   b. $|2x - 1| < -5$
   c. $|2x - 1| > 5$
   d. $|2x - 1| > -5$

4. $|2x-5|=3$ *[handwritten: $2x-5=3$]*   5. $|x+1|\geq 3$

     a. $x=-1$ or 1   *[handwritten: $2x-5=-3$]*
     b. $x=1$ or 4 *(circled)*
     c. $x=4$ or -4
     d. $x=-1$ or 4   *[handwritten: $x=4$]*

         a. $x\leq -4$ and $x\geq 2$
         b. $x\geq -4$ and $x\leq 2$
         c. $x\geq -4$ or $x\leq 2$
         d. $x\leq -4$ or $x\geq 2$

[handwritten: $x=1$]

6. $|2x+5|\leq 11$

     a. $x\leq -8$ and $x\leq 3$
     b. $-8\leq x\leq 3$
     c. $-3\leq x\leq 3$
     d. $x\leq -3$ and $x\leq 3$

7. $|x-1|+6=8$

         a. $x=3$ or -13
         b. $x=-1$ or -13
         c. $x=-1$ or 3
         d. $\emptyset$

[handwritten: $3x+6>-9$]

[handwritten: $x<-5$]

8. $|2x-1|+3<6$

     a. $-1<x<2$
     b. $-4<x<2$
     c. $-4<x<-1$
     d. $-2<x2$

9. $|3x+6|-5>4$

         a. $x<\dfrac{-5}{3}$ or $x>1$

         b. $x>\dfrac{-5}{3}$ or $x<1$

         c. $x<-5$ or $x>1$ *(circled)*
         d. $x>-5$ or $x>1$

[handwritten: -6 -6]

[handwritten: $3x+6=9$]

10. $-2|x|+5=7$

     a. $x=-1$ or 1
     b. $x=-6$ or 6
     c. $x=-1$
     d. $\emptyset$ *(circled)*

[handwritten: -5 -5]

[handwritten: $-2|x|+5=7$]

[handwritten: $3x=3$ $3x+6=-$]

[handwritten: $\dfrac{3x}{3}$ 3]

[handwritten: $\dfrac{-2|x|}{-2}=\dfrac{2}{-2}$]

[handwritten: $x=1$]

[handwritten: $x=-1$]

[handwritten: $|x|=-1$ $x=-1$]

[handwritten: $x=1$]

Content Cluster: ALGEBRA - Section 4

Objective: Students will simplify expressions prior to solving linear equations and inequalities with one variable.

> **Parent Tip:** Distribute to eliminate all parentheses. Add the coefficients of the like terms.
>
> **EXAMPLE:** $3(2x+5)-4x+3$ becomes $6x+15-4x+3$ and simplifies to $2x+18$.

Simplify the following expressions.

1. $4(2x-5)+6x$

   a. $14x-5$
   b. $12x-20$
   c. $14x-20$
   d. $2x-20$

2. $-3(x-2)-(2x+3)$

   a. $-5x+9$
   b. $-5x+3$
   c. $x+3$
   d. $x-9$

3. $2(3x+4)+3(x+5)$

   a. $8x+23$
   b. $9x+9$
   c. $9x+13$
   d. $9x+23$

4. $-2(x+5)-7$

   a. $2x-17$
   b. $-2x-17$
   c. $-2x+3$
   d. $-2x-3$

5. $3(2+4(3x-2))$

   a. $36x-18$
   b. $36x-24$
   c. $36x$
   d. $36x+18$

6. $-(2x-1)+3(x+4)-2(x+2)$

   a. $3x+9$
   b. $x+9$
   c. $-x+9$
   d. $-x+7$

> **Parent Tip:** When solving equations or inequalities, simplify the expressions on each side. Use opposite operations to solve for the variable. Don't forget the property for multiplying or dividing an inequality by a negative number. The inequality changes to its opposite.
>
> **EXAMPLE:** $-2x > 6$ becomes $\dfrac{-2x}{-2} < \dfrac{6}{-2}$ and simplifies to x<-3.

Solve for the equation or inequality for problems 7-12.

7. $-3(x+5)-6 \geq 9$

     a. $x \geq -10$
     b. $x \geq 10$
     c. $x \leq 10$
     d. $x \leq -10$

10. $3(4x-1)+5(x-4)=2$

     a. $x = \dfrac{25}{17}$
     b. $x = \dfrac{23}{17}$
     c. $x = \dfrac{9}{17}$
     d. $x = \dfrac{14}{17}$

8. $2(3x+5)=4(x-3)$

     a. $x = -11$
     b. $x = -1$
     c. $x = 11$
     d. $x = \dfrac{-11}{5}$

11. $\dfrac{-x+3}{5} \leq 6$

     a. $x \leq -27$
     b. $x \leq 33$
     c. $x \geq -27$
     d. $x \geq 33$

9. $2x+5(x-3) < 3(3x-5)$

     a. $x > -15$
     b. $x > 0$
     c. $x < 0$
     d. $x < -15$

12. $-2(x+1)-3(2x-5) > 6$

     a. $x < \dfrac{-23}{8}$
     b. $x > \dfrac{-23}{8}$
     c. $x < \dfrac{7}{8}$
     d. $x > \dfrac{7}{8}$

Content Cluster: ALGEBRA - Section 5

Objective: Students will solve multi-step problems, including word problems, involving linear equations and linear inequalities that include justification of steps.

Parent Tip: Word problems are usually the most challenging problems for students to conquer. Try to have students make a chart or representation of the unknowns. It is important to know some of the basic geometry formulas for perimeters of rectangles (P=2l+2w) or squares (P=4s). The next step involves writing an equation and solving the equation. When the answer is found, ask yourself if the answer makes sense. Some word problems might involve a direct translation of English words into math symbols. A thorough understanding of the vocabulary of math terminology will be necessary for success.

Find the equation for problems 1-8.

1. Twice the sum of a number and five is ten.

   a. $2x+5=10$
   b. $2x-5=10$
   c. $2(x-5)=10$
   d. $2(x+5)=10$

2. The length of a rectangle is three less than four times the width. The perimeter is twenty inches.

   a. $4x-3+x=20$
   b. $2(4x-3)+x=20$
   c. $2(4x-3)+2x=20$
   d. $2(3-4x)+2x=20$

3. The sum of three consecutive odd integers is thirty-nine.

   a. $x+(x+2)+(x+4)=39$
   b. $x+(x+1)+(x+3)=39$
   c. $x+(x+1)+(x+2)=39$
   d. $x+(x+1)+(x+5)=39$

4. Five subtracted from a number is four times the difference of the number and two.

    a. $5 - x = 4(x - 2)$
    b. $5 - x = 4(x + 2)$
    c. $x - 5 = 4(x + 2)$
    d. $x - 5 = 4(x - 2)$

5. The length of a rectangle is one less than three times the width. The area is thirty square feet.

    a. $2(3x - 1) + 2x = 30$
    b. $(3x - 1)x = 30$
    c. $(1 - 3x)(x) = 30$
    d. $(3x - 1) + x = 30$

6. Five times a number is less than six more than twice the number.

    a. $5x + 6 > 2x$
    b. $6 - 5x > 2x$
    c. $5x < 6 + 2x$
    d. $5x < 2x - 6$

7. The sum of three consecutive integers is at least forty-five.

    a. $x + (x + 2) + (x + 4) \geq 45$
    b. $x + (x + 1) + (x + 2) > 45$
    c. $x + (x + 1) + (x + 2) \leq 45$
    d. $x + (x + 1) + (x + 2) \geq 45$

8. Twice a number less than two is ten more than three times the number.

    a. $2x - 2 = 10 + 3x$
    b. $2 - 2x = 10 + 3x$
    c. $2x < 2 + 10 + 3x$
    d. $2 - 2x = 3x - 10$

Parent Tip: When using multi-steps to solve equations or inequalities, the properties involved will include the properties of equality. Many algebra books include a summary page of these properties.

9. If $3x = 15$, then $\dfrac{3x}{3} = \dfrac{15}{3}$. Why?

    a. Addition Property
    b. Subtraction Property
    c. Multiplication Property
    d. Division Property

10. If $3x - 5 = 11$, then $3x - 5 + 5 = 11 + 5$. Why?

    a. Addition Property
    b. Subtraction Property
    c. Multiplication Property
    d. Division Property

11. If $6 = 2x - 7$, then $2x - 7 = 6$. Why?

    a. Reflexive Property
    b. Symmetric Property
    c. Transitive Property
    d. Identity Property

12. If $3x - 11 = 18$ and $18 = 2x + 15$, then $3x - 11 = 2x + 15$. Why?

    a. Reflexive Property
    b. Symmetric Property
    c. Transitive Property
    d. Identity Property

Content Cluster: ALGEBRA - Section 6

Objective: Students will graph linear equations and inequalities, and find the x- and y- intercepts of equations.

Parent Tip: Try to get the equation into the form $y = mx + b$ where m = slope and b = y-intercept or the form $Ax + By = C$ where $m = \dfrac{-A}{B}$ and $b = \dfrac{C}{B}$. Try to find the slope and y-intercept. Plot the y-intercept on the y-axis and use the slope (rise over the run) to find a second point to graph the line.

EXAMPLE: $3x + 4y = 8.$ $m = \dfrac{-3}{4}, b = 2$

Plot the point (0,2) on the y-axis. Rise –3 and run 4 to find the second point to graph the line.

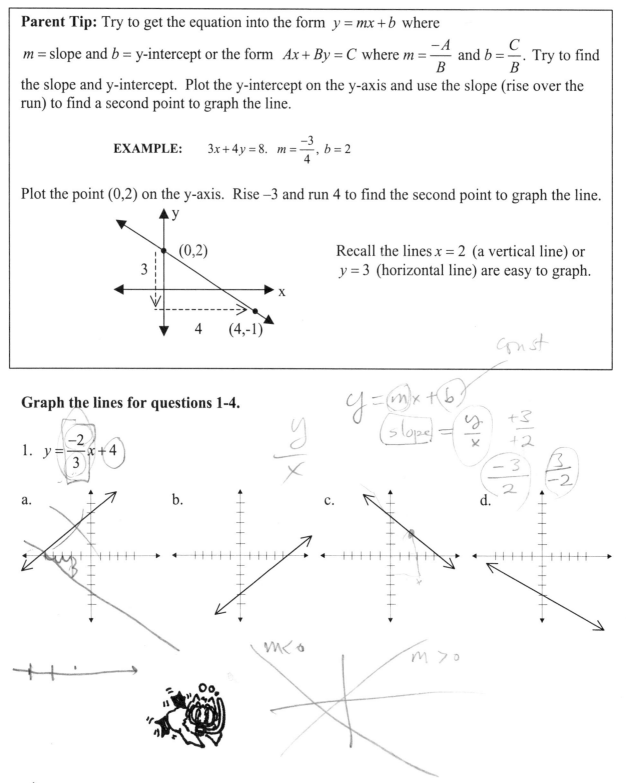

Recall the lines $x = 2$ (a vertical line) or $y = 3$ (horizontal line) are easy to graph.

Graph the lines for questions 1-4.

1. $y = \dfrac{-2}{3}x + 4$

a.   b.   c.   d.

y = 3x − 1

2. $3x - y = 1$

a.   b.   c.   d.

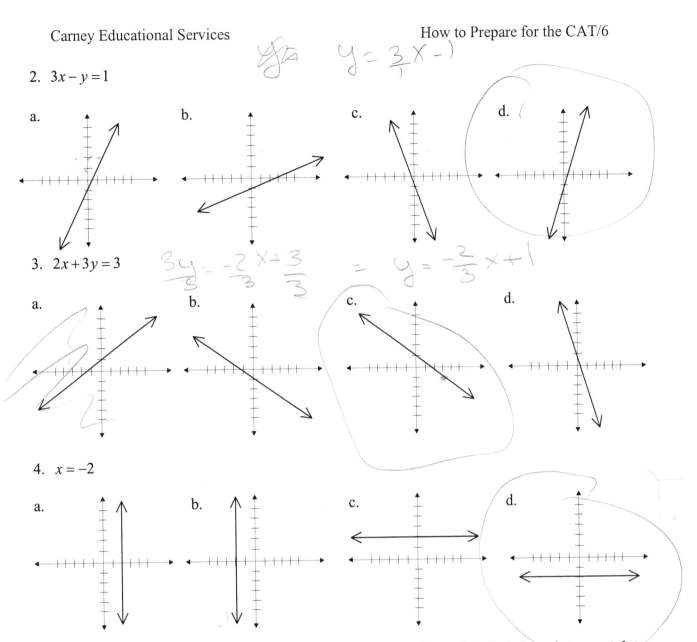

3. $2x + 3y = 3$

$3y = -2x + 3$ $= y = \frac{-2}{3}x + 1$
$\frac{3y}{3} = \frac{-2x}{3} + \frac{3}{3}$

a.   b.   c.   d.

4. $x = -2$

a.   b.   c.   d.

To find the x-intercept of an equation, let y = 0 and solve for x. To find the y-intercept, let x = 0 and solve for y.

5. Find the x-intercept for $3x + 2y = -12$.

a. 6   b. −6   c. 4   d. −4

6. Find the y-intercept for $x - 3y = 6$.

a. −2   b. 2   c. 6   d. −6

7. Find the sum of the x- and the y-intercepts for $y = 2x - 5$.

a. −5   b. $-\frac{5}{2}$ c. $\frac{5}{2}$ d. $-\frac{15}{2}$

$y \leq 2x - 1$

> **Parent Tip:** To graph inequalities, graph the line remembering to make it a dotted line if it is a < or > sign. Choose a point on one side of the line to determine if the inequality is true (the shaded side) or false (the non-shaded side).

8. Graph $2x - y \geq 1$

$-y \geq 2x + 1$ $y \leq 2x + -1$ $2x - 1 \geq y$

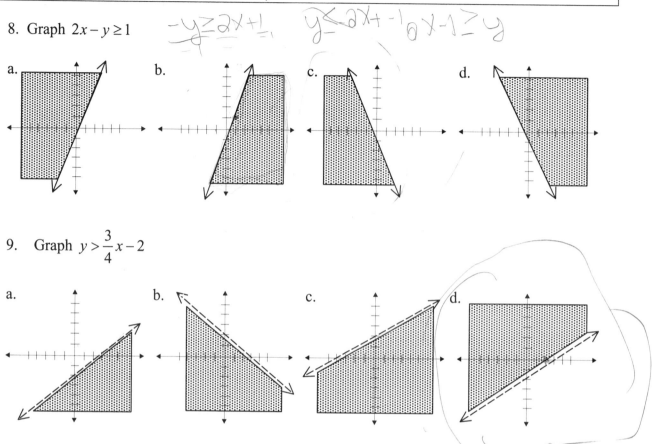

a.   b.   c.   d.

9.   Graph $y > \dfrac{3}{4}x - 2$

a.   b.   c.   d.

10. Graph $x + 3y \leq 0$

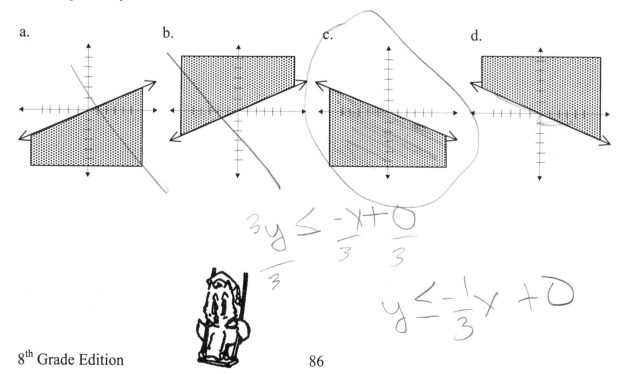

a.   b.   c.   d.

$\dfrac{3y}{3} \leq \dfrac{-x}{3} + \dfrac{0}{3}$

$y \leq -\dfrac{1}{3}x + 0$

Carney Educational Services

How to Prepare for the CAT/6
Howard, Yale, Princeton, Stanford, MIT.

Content Cluster: ALGEBRA - Section 7

Objective: Students will verify that a point lies on a line given an equation. Students will find the equation of a line using the point-slope formula.

Parent Tip: Given a point (x, y), substitute the values to see if the equation is true.

Choose the correct answer.

1. (4, -3) lies on which line?

   a. $2x + y = 11$
   b. $3x - y = 15$
   c. $x - 2y = -2$
   d. $x + y = -1$

2. The point (-2, -1) does **not** lie on which line?

   a. $3x - y = -5$
   b. $x - y = -1$
   c. $2x + 3y = -7$
   d. $-x + 2y = -4$

3. Find the point that lies on the line $y = -3x - 5$.

   a. (3, -14)
   b. (2, 1)
   c. (-1, 2)
   d. (-2, -1)

4. Find the point that does **not** lie on the line $x - 3y = 5$.

   a. (14, 3)
   b. (-1, -2)
   c. (8, 1)
   d. (7, -4)

The point slope formula is $(y - y_1) = m(x - x_1)$ where m is the slope and the point (x_1, y_1) is substituted in the formula. Use the algebra properties to write the equation in the form $Ax + By = C$.

5. Find the equation of a line if the slope is $-\dfrac{3}{4}$ and passing through the point (-1, 2).

    a. $4x + 3y = 2$
    b. $3x - 4y = -1$
    c. $3x + 4y = 5$
    d. $4x - 3y = -10$

6. Find the equation of a line if the slope is 2 and passing through the point (5, -3).

    a. $2x + y = 7$
    b. $2x + y = 13$
    c. $2x - y = 13$
    d. $2x - y = 7$

7. Find the equation of a line passing through the points (4, -2), (-1, 1).

    a. $3x - 5y = 22$
    b. $3x + 5y = 2$
    c. $3x + 5y = -2$
    d. $x - 5y = 14$

8. Find the equation of a line if the slope is $\dfrac{2}{3}$ and passing through (4, -1).

    a. $2x - 3y = 11$
    b. $3x - 2y = 14$
    c. $2x + 3y = 5$
    d. $3x + 2y = 10$

Content Cluster: ALGEBRA - Section 8

Objective: Students will understand the relationship of the slopes for parallel lines and perpendicular lines. Students will find the equation of a line perpendicular or parallel to a given line that passes through a given point.

Parent Tip: Parallel lines have equal slopes. The slopes of perpendicular lines will be negative reciprocals of each other or the product of their slopes will equal -1.

Questions 1 – 6 determine if the lines are parallel, perpendicular, or neither.

1. $y = 3x + 4$
    $x + 3y = 2$ $\frac{3y}{3} = -\frac{1}{3}x + \frac{2}{3}$

    a. parallel
    b. perpendicular
    c. neither

2. $y = \frac{2}{3}x - 1$
    $2x + 3y = 6$

    a. parallel
    b. perpendicular
    c. neither

3. $4x - 2y = 8$
    $2x - y = 3$

    a. parallel
    b. perpendicular
    c. neither

4. $y = -\frac{1}{2}x + 5$
    $y = 2x - 1$

    a. parallel
    b. perpendicular
    c. neither

5. $3x + y = 6$
   $y = -3x - 2$

    a. parallel
    b. perpendicular
    c. neither

6. $x - y = 4$
   $-x + y = 2$

    a. parallel
    b. perpendicular
    c. neither

Parent Tip: Remember to find the equation of a line, a point and a slope is needed. Substitute the point and the slope in the point-slope formula.

---

7. Find the equation of a line that is perpendicular to the line $3x - 2y = 6$ and passing through the point (-1, 4).

    a. $3x - 2y = -11$ c. $2x + 3y = 10$
    b. $3x + 2y = 5$ d. $2x - 3y = -14$

8. Find the equation of a line that is perpendicular to the line $y = 4x - 3$ and passing through the point (2, 3).

    a. $4x + y = 11$ c. $x + 4y = 14$
    b. $4x - y = 5$ d. $x - 4y = -10$

9. Find the equation of a line that is parallel to the line $4x + 5y = 10$ and passing through the point (1, -3).

    a. $4x + 5y = -11$ c. $4x - 5y = 19$
    b. $5x + 4y = -18$ d. $5x - 4y = 17$

10. Find the equation of a line that is parallel to the line $y = -\dfrac{2}{5}x + 1$ and passing through the point (-2, 4).

    a. $2x - 5y = -24$ c. $2x + 5y = 24$
    b. $5x - 2y = -18$ d. $2x + 5y = 16$

Content Cluster: ALGEBRA - Section 9

Objective: Students will solve two linear equations in two variables algebraically. Students will interpret the answer graphically. Students will solve a system of two linear inequalities and sketch the solution sets.

Parent Tip: To solve two linear equations algebraically, try to use one of two methods. The first method called substitution is best to use when a variable is easy to solve in one of the two equations.

Example: $x = 3y + 4$, $5x - 2y = 3$

Since x is solved for in the first equation, substitute in the second equation; $5(3y + 4) - 2y = 3$. Solve for y. Substitute the y value to find x. Write the answer as an ordered pair (1, -1). The second method called addition-subtraction method is best to use when both equations are in standard form. Try to get the coefficients of one variable the same or its opposite.

Example: $x - 3y = 4$, $4x + y = 3$

Multiply the second equation by 3 creates the two equations as $x - 3y = 4$ and $12x + 3y = 9$. Add the equations to get $13x = 13$. Solve for x, and substitute to find y getting the answer of (1, -1).

Solve questions 1-4 algebraically.

1. $3x - y = 9$ and $x - y = 5$

    a. $(\frac{7}{2}, \frac{-3}{2})$
    b. (7, 2)
    c. (1, -6)
    d. (2, -3)

2. $x = 2y - 1$ and $2x - 3y = -4$

    a. (-3, -7)
    b. (-5, -2)
    c. (3, 5)
    d. (2, 3)

3. $4x + 3y = 5$ and $2x - 5y = 9$

    a. (-2, 1)
    b. (-2, -1)
    c. (2, -1)
    d. (5, 5)

4. $3x + 2y = 10$ and $y = -4x + 15$

    a. (2, -2)
    b. (4, -1)
    c. (-3, 3)
    d. (-1, 4)

Parent Tip: To solve linear equations by graphing, graph the two equations to find a point in common.

Solve questions 5 and 6 by graphing.

5. $y = -x + 2$ and $3x - y = -2$

a.   b.   c.   d.

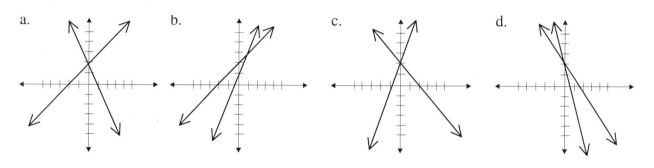

6. $x - y = -3$ and $y = -x - 1$

a.   b.   c.   d.

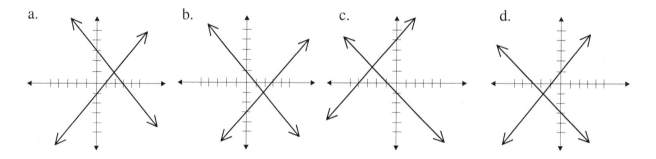

Parent Tip: To solve two linear inequalities by graphing, graph each inequality on the graph. The intersection of their shaded areas will consist of the sketch of the solution set.

Solve questions 7 and 8 by graphing.

7. $y \geq \dfrac{-1}{2}x + 2$ and $2x + y \leq -1$

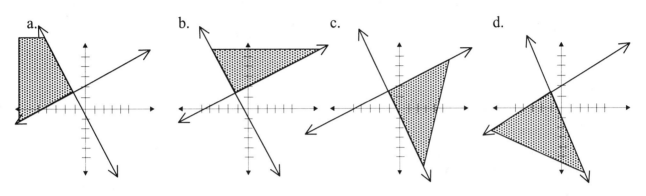

a.   b.   c.   d.

8. $y \geq -3x$ and $x - y \geq 3$

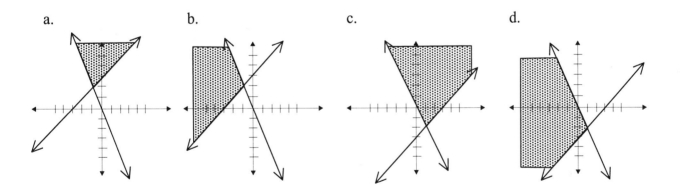

a.   b.   c.   d.

Content Cluster: ALGEBRA - Section 10

Objective: Students will add, subtract, multiply, and divide monomials and polynomials. Students will solve multi-step problems, including word problems, using these techniques.

Parent Tip: When adding or subtracting polynomials, combine the coefficients of the like terms.

Example: $(3x-5)+(4x+2)$ simplifies to $7x-3$.

When multiplying monomials, multiply numbers with numbers and variables with variables.

Example: $(4x^2)(2x^5)$ simplifies to $8x^7$.

When multiplying two binomials, use the FOIL (First-Outside-Inside-Last) process. When dividing monomials, divide numbers with numbers and variables with variables.

Simplify the polynomial expressions for questions 1-9.

1. $(5x-7)+(2x+3)$

    a. $7x-10$
    b. $3x-4$
    c. $3x-10$
    d. $7x-4$

2. $(3x^6)(2x^3)$

    a. $6x^{18}$
    b. $5x^{18}$
    c. $6x^9$
    d. $5x^9$

3. $(7x+5)-(9x-4)$

    a. $-2x+9$
    b. $-2x+1$
    c. $2x+9$
    d. $2x+1$

4. $\dfrac{9x^3+6x^2}{3x^2}$

    a. $3x+3$
    b. $3x+2x$
    c. $6x+2$
    d. $3x+2$

5. $6x^2+8x^2$

    a. $14x^4$
    b. $14x^2$
    c. $48x^2$
    d. $2x^2$

6. $(3x-4)(2x+1)$

    a. $6x^2+5x-4$
    b. $6x^2-5x+4$
    c. $6x^2+11x-4$
    d. $6x^2-5x-4$

7. $\dfrac{15x^3 - 10x^2 + 5x}{5x}$

    a. $3x^2 - 2x$
    b. $10x^2 - 5x + 1$
    c. $3x^2 - 2x + 1$
    d. $3x^2 - 2x + x$

8. $(-2x^3)(-x^2)$

    a. $2x^5$
    b. $2x^6$
    c. $-2x^6$
    d. $-2x^5$

9. $-3x^2(2x^3 + 5x^2 - 1)$

    a. $-6x^5 - 15x^4 + 3x^2$
    b. $-6x^5 + 15x^4 + 3x^2$
    c. $-6x^6 - 15x^4 + 3x^2$
    d. $-6x^6 - 15x^4 - 3x^2$

The following word problems begin with polynomial expressions. After simplifying the polynomials using the arithmetic operations, choose the best equation for each problem.

10. The sum of three consecutive even integers is twenty-six.

    a. $3x + 3 = 26$
    b. $3x + 6 = 26$
    c. $3x + 8 = 26$
    d. $3x + 4 = 26$

11. The length of a rectangle is three more than twice the width of a rectangle. The area is sixty-five square feet.

    a. $2x^2 - 3x = 65$
    b. $2x^2 - 3 = 65$
    c. $2x^2 + 3 = 65$
    d. $2x^2 + 3x = 65$

12. The length of a rectangle is two less than five times the width of a rectangle. The perimeter is thirty-two inches.

    a. $6x - 2 = 32$
    b. $6x + 2 = 32$
    c. $12x - 4 = 32$
    d. $12x + 4 = 32$

Content Cluster: ALGEBRA - Section 11

Objective: Students will apply basic factoring techniques to second and simple third degree polynomials. This includes finding a common factor to all terms in a polynomial and recognizing the difference of two squares and perfect squares of binomials.

Parent Tip: Look to see if each term of the polynomial has a common factor.

Example: $9x^3 - 12x^2 + 6x$ has a greatest common factor of $3x$.

Check the binomials to see if they are in the form $a^2 - b^2$ which factors to $(a+b)(a-b)$. Factor the trinomials into two binomials.

Example: $3x^2 - 7x - 6$ factors to $(3x+2)(x-3)$.

If the trinomial is a perfect square $(a^2 + 2ab + b^2)$, it factors to $(a+b)^2$.

Factor completely and choose the correct answer.

1. $x^2 + 10x - 24$

    a. $(x+6)(x-4)$
    b. $(x+6)(x+4)$
    c. $(x-12)(x+2)$
    d. $(x+12)(x-2)$

2. $3x^2 - 6x$

    a. $3x(x-3)$
    b. $3x(x-2)$
    c. $x(3x-6)$
    d. $3(x^2 - 2x)$

3. $6x^2 + x - 12$

    a. $(3x-4)(2x+3)$
    b. $(3x+4)(2x-3)$
    c. $(6x+3)(x-2)$
    d. $(3x-4)(2x-3)$

4. $9x^2 - 64$

    a. $(3x-8)^2$
    b. $(3x+8)^2$
    c. $(3x-16)(3x+4)$
    d. $(3x+8)(3x-8)$

5. $x^2 - 5x + 6$

    a. $(x-6)(x+1)$
    b. $(x+6)(x-1)$
    c. $(x-3)(x-2)$
    d. $(x+3)(x+2)$

6. $4x^2 + 20x + 25$

    a. $(4x+5)^2$
    b. $(2x+5)^2$
    c. $(2x+5)(2x-5)$
    d. $2(x+5)^2$

7. $2x^3 + 12x^2 + 16x$

    a. $(2x^2 + 8x)(x + 2)$
    b. $(x + 4)(2x^2 + 4x)$
    c. $2x(x + 2)^2$
    d. $2x(x + 4)(x + 2)$

8. $3x^3 - 12x$

    a. $3x(x^2 - 4)$
    b. $3x(x + 2)^2$
    c. $3x(x + 2)(x - 2)$
    d. $3x(x - 2)^2$

9. $x^2 - 2x - 8$

    a. $(x - 4)(x + 2)$
    b. $(x + 4)(x - 2)$
    c. $2(x - 2)(x + 1)$
    d. $(x - 4)^2$

10. Which of the following does **not** factor into a difference of two squares?

    a. $4x^2 - 25$
    b. $2x^2 - 9$
    c. $x^2 - 16$
    d. $9x^2 - 4y^2$

11. Which of the following does **not** factor into a difference of two squares?

    a. $x^2 - y^5$
    b. $x^2 - y^4$
    c. $9x^2 - 1$
    d. $y^6 - x^4$

12. Which of the following does **not** factor into a perfect square?

    a. $x^2 + 6x + 9$
    b. $4x^2 - 20x + 25$
    c. $9x^2 + 24x + 16$
    d. $x^2 - 4x - 4$

13. Which of the following does **not** factor into a perfect square?

    a. $x^2 - 20x + 100$
    b. $4x^2 - 4x + 1$
    c. $4x^2 + 6x + 9$
    d. $x^2 - 4xy + 4y^2$

Content Cluster: ALGEBRA - Section 12

Objective: Students will simplify fractions with polynomials in the numerator and denominator by factoring both and reducing to lowest terms.

Parent Tip: Factor completely the numerator and the denominator. Reduce monomials with monomials. Reduce binomials with binomials. **NEVER** reduce a monomial with part of a binomial.

Example: $\dfrac{3(x+4)}{x+4} = 3$ but $\dfrac{x+3}{3} \neq x+1$.

Simplify the following fractions.

1. $\dfrac{x^2-5x}{x^2-25}$

   a. $\dfrac{x}{5}$
   b. $\dfrac{x}{x+5}$
   c. $\dfrac{1}{5}$
   d. $\dfrac{1}{x-5}$

2. $\dfrac{x^2-5x+6}{x^2-6x+8}$

   a. $\dfrac{3}{4}$
   b. $\dfrac{x-3}{x+4}$
   c. $\dfrac{x+3}{x+4}$
   d. $\dfrac{x-3}{x-4}$

3. $\dfrac{2x^2-6x}{4x-12}$

   a. $\dfrac{x}{2}$
   b. $\dfrac{x}{4}$
   c. $\dfrac{x-3}{2}$
   d. $\dfrac{1}{2}$

4. $\dfrac{x^2-x}{3x}$

   a. $\dfrac{x^2-1}{3}$
   b. $\dfrac{x-1}{3}$
   c. $\dfrac{x}{3}$
   d. $\dfrac{1}{3}$

5. $\dfrac{x^2+2x-24}{x^2-2x-8}$

   a. 3
   b. $\dfrac{x+6}{x+2}$
   c. $\dfrac{x-6}{x-2}$
   d. $\dfrac{x+6}{x-2}$

6. $\dfrac{x^2-9}{x^2+6x+9}$

   a. $\dfrac{1}{6x}$
   b. $\dfrac{1}{x+3}$
   c. $\dfrac{x-3}{x+3}$
   d. -1

Content Cluster: ALGEBRA - Section 13

Objective: Students will add, subtract, multiply, and divide rational expressions and functions.　Students will solve both computationally and conceptually challenging problems using these techniques.

> **Parent Tip:** When adding or subtracting rational expressions, the denominators must be the same before the expressions are combined. When multiplying rational expressions, factor the numerator and denominator completely and reduce before the expressions are multiplied. When dividing rational expressions, multiply the first fraction by the reciprocal of the second fraction by using the techniques for multiplying rational expressions.

Simplify the expressions.

1. $\dfrac{3x-5}{x^2+5x-6} - \dfrac{x-3}{x^2+5x-6}$

   a. $\dfrac{2x-8}{x^2+5x-6}$

   b. $\dfrac{2}{x+6}$

   c. $\dfrac{2x-2}{x^2+5x-6}$

   d. $\dfrac{2}{x-6}$

2. $\dfrac{x^2-10x-24}{x^2-4} \cdot \dfrac{x^2+x-6}{x^2+7x+12}$

   a. -3

   b. $\dfrac{(x-6)(x-4)}{x+4}$

   c. $x-6$

   d. $\dfrac{x-12}{x+4}$

3. $\dfrac{5}{x+3} + \dfrac{3}{x+2}$

   a. $\dfrac{8x+19}{(x+3)(x+2)}$

   b. $\dfrac{8}{2x+5}$

   c. $\dfrac{2(4x+9)}{(x+3)(x+2)}$

   d. $\dfrac{8}{(x+3)(x+2)}$

4. $\dfrac{x^2-1}{3x-6} \div \dfrac{4x-4}{x^2-4}$

   a. $\dfrac{4(x+1)}{3(x+2)}$

   b. $\dfrac{4(x+1)}{x+2}$

   c. $\dfrac{4(x+1)}{3}$

   d. $\dfrac{(x+1)(x+2)}{12}$

5. $\dfrac{6x+12}{3x-9} \cdot \dfrac{9-x^2}{2x^2+10x+12}$

     a.   1
     b. -1
     c.   0
     d. $\dfrac{2}{x+2}$

6. $\dfrac{4x}{x^2-25} - \dfrac{2}{x-5}$

     a. $\dfrac{4x-2}{x^2-25}$
     b. $\dfrac{4x}{x-5}$
     c. $\dfrac{2}{x+5}$
     d. $\dfrac{2}{x-5}$

7. $\dfrac{3}{10x} + \dfrac{6}{5x^2}$

     a. $\dfrac{3(x+4)}{10x^2}$
     b. $\dfrac{3(x+2)}{5x^2}$
     c. $\dfrac{9}{10x^2}$
     d. $\dfrac{15x^2+60x}{50x^3}$

8. $\dfrac{6x^3y}{25y^2} \cdot \dfrac{20}{12xy}$

     a. $\dfrac{2x^3}{5y^2}$
     b. $\dfrac{4x^2}{5y^2}$
     c. $\dfrac{2x^2}{5y^2}$
     d. $\dfrac{x^2}{5y^2}$

Content Cluster: ALGEBRA - Section 14

Objective: Students will solve a quadratic equation by factoring or completing the square.

Parent Tip: To solve a quadratic equation by factoring, the student must get the equation in the form $ax^2 + bx + c = 0$. Factor the polynomial completely. Recall the fact that if $ab = 0$, then $a = 0$ or $b = 0$. Separate and solve for each root.

Example: $2x^2 + x - 3 = 0$

The equation factors to $(2x + 3)(x - 1) = 0$. It separates to $2x + 3 = 0$ or $x - 1 = 0$.

The roots are $-\dfrac{2}{3}$, 1.

Solve by factoring for questions 1 – 6.

1. $3x^2 - 2x - 8 = 0$

   a. $x = \dfrac{-4}{3}$, 2

   b. $x = \dfrac{4}{3}$, 2

   c. $x = \dfrac{-4}{3}$, -2

   d. $x = \dfrac{4}{3}$, -2

2. $x^2 - 16 = 0$

   a. $x = 16, -16$

   b. $x = 4, -4$

   c. $x = 4$

   d. $x = -4$

3. $4x^2 - 20x + 25 = 0$

   a. $x = 5, -5$

   b. $x = \dfrac{5}{2}, \dfrac{-5}{2}$

   c. $x = \dfrac{5}{2}$

   d. $x = \dfrac{-5}{2}$

4. $x^2 - 3x - 4 = -6$

   a. $x = -4, 1$

   b. $x = 1, 2$

   c. $x = -1, -2$

   d. $x = -1, 4$

5. $3x^2 - 5x = 0$

   a. $x = \dfrac{5}{3}$

   b. $x = \dfrac{-5}{3}, \dfrac{5}{3}$

   c. $x = 0, \dfrac{-5}{3}$

   d. $x = 0, \dfrac{5}{3}$

6. $x^2 - 10x = 24$

   a. $x = 4, 6$

   b. $x = -4, -6$

   c. $x = -2, 12$

   d. $x = -12, 2$

nt Tip: To solve a quadratic equation by completing the square involves a multi-step cess. Have students practice with equations in form $x^2 + bx + c = 0$ before advancing to uations in the form $ax^2 + bx + c = 0$. When completing the square it is important to get the coefficient of the x^2 term to be 1.

Solve for x by completing the square for $ax^2 + bx + c = 0$.

Transform the equation to $ax^2 + bx = -c$.

Divide all terms by a forming $x^2 + \dfrac{b}{a}x = \dfrac{-c}{a}$.

Recall the binomial formulas $(a+b)^2 = a^2 + 2ab + b^2$ and $(a-b)^2 = a^2 - 2ab + b^2$.

Compare the expressions: $x^2 + \dfrac{b}{a}x$ and $a^2 + 2ab + b^2$

$a = x$, add $b^2 = \dfrac{b^2}{4a^2}$ to both sides. $x^2 + \dfrac{b}{a}x + \dfrac{b^2}{4a^2} = \dfrac{b^2}{4a^2} + \dfrac{-c}{a}$

Factor $(x + \dfrac{b}{2a})^2 = \dfrac{b^2 - 4ac}{4a^2}$

Square root both sides $x + \dfrac{b}{2a} = \dfrac{\pm\sqrt{b^2 - 4ac}}{2a}$

Solve for x $x = \dfrac{-b \pm \sqrt{b^2 - 4ac}}{2a}$

Example: $x^2 + 6x - 4 = 0$. $x^2 + 6x = 4$ where $a = x$ and $b = 3$. Add b^2 to both sides to form $x^2 + 6x + 9 = 9 + 4$ or $(x+3)^2 = 13$. Solve for x where $x + 3 = \pm\sqrt{13}$ and transforming to $x = -3 \pm \sqrt{13}$.

Example: $2x^2 - 5x + 1 = 0$

$x^2 - \dfrac{5}{2}x = \dfrac{-1}{2}$ where $a = x$ and $b = \dfrac{5}{4}$.

Add $\dfrac{25}{16}$ to both sides to form $x^2 - \dfrac{5}{2}x + \dfrac{25}{16} = \dfrac{25}{16} + \dfrac{-1}{2}$ or $(x - \dfrac{5}{4})^2 = \dfrac{17}{16}$.

Solve for x where $x - \dfrac{5}{4} = \dfrac{\pm\sqrt{17}}{4}$ and $x = \dfrac{5 \pm \sqrt{17}}{4}$.

For questions 7 – 9, what number must you divide by?

7. $3x^2 + 8x - 2 = 0$

    a. 2
    b. 8
    c. 3
    d. −2

8. $5x^2 - 7x + 1 = 0$

    a. 1
    b. 7
    c. −7
    d. 5

9. $2x^2 - 3x - 6 = 0$

    a. 1
    b. 2
    c. 3
    d. 6

For questions 10 – 12, what number must you add to both sides?

10. $x^2 - \dfrac{5}{3}x = 2$

    a. $\dfrac{25}{9}$
    b. $\dfrac{5}{3}$
    c. $\dfrac{25}{36}$
    d. $\dfrac{-25}{36}$

11. $x^2 + 6x = 8$

    a. 9
    b. 36
    c. −9
    d. −36

12. $x^2 - \dfrac{3}{4} = \dfrac{1}{2}$

    a. $\dfrac{9}{16}$
    b. $\dfrac{-9}{16}$
    c. $\dfrac{-9}{64}$
    d. $\dfrac{9}{64}$

For questions 13 – 15, solve by completing the square.

13. $x^2 - 6x - 2 = 0$

    a. $x = 3 \pm \sqrt{11}$
    b. $x = -3 \pm \sqrt{11}$
    c. $x = 3 \pm \sqrt{7}$
    d. $x = -3 \pm \sqrt{7}$

14. $3x^2 + 5x - 1 = 0$

    a. $x = \dfrac{-5 \pm \sqrt{13}}{6}$
    b. $x = \dfrac{5 \pm \sqrt{13}}{6}$
    c. $x = \dfrac{-5 \pm \sqrt{37}}{6}$
    d. $x = \dfrac{5 \pm \sqrt{37}}{6}$

15. $x^2 + 4x - 8 = 0$

    a. $x = 2 \pm 2\sqrt{2}$
    b. $x = 2 \pm 2\sqrt{3}$
    c. $x = -2 \pm 2\sqrt{2}$
    d. $x = -2 \pm 2\sqrt{3}$

Content Cluster: ALGEBRA - Section 15

Objective: Students will apply algebraic techniques to rate problems, work problems, and percent mixture problems.

> **Parent Tip:** Motion problems can be solved using the formulas (Rate)(Time)=Distance or RT=D. Recall $R=\dfrac{D}{T}$ and $T=\dfrac{D}{R}$.

Choose the correct equation for the following word problems.

1. Two trains leave in opposite directions at the same time. If the speeds of the two trains are 60 mph and 75 mph, when will they be 505 miles apart?

    a. $75x - 60x = 505$

    b. $\dfrac{75x}{505} - \dfrac{60x}{505} = 1$

    c. $75x + 60x = 505$

    d. $\dfrac{75}{x} + \dfrac{60}{x} = 505$

2. The average speed on a highway is 20 mph less than the freeway. If it takes the same time to travel 125 miles on the highway as it takes to go 175 miles on the freeway, find the average speed on the highway.

    a. $\dfrac{x + x + 20}{125} = 175$

    b. $\dfrac{125}{x} = \dfrac{175}{x - 20}$

    c. $\dfrac{125}{x + 20} = \dfrac{175}{x}$

    d. $\dfrac{125}{x - 20} = \dfrac{175}{x}$

3. A boat travels in still water at a rate of 10 mph. A round trip down the river for 21 miles and back takes 5 hours. Find the rate of the current.

    a. $\dfrac{21}{10 + x} + \dfrac{21}{10 - x} = 5$

    b. $\dfrac{21}{10 + x} - \dfrac{21}{10 - x} = 5$

    c. $\dfrac{10 + x}{21} + \dfrac{10 - x}{21} = 5$

    d. $\dfrac{10 + x}{21} - \dfrac{10 - x}{21} = 5$

Parent Tip: Work word problems involve the rate (amount of the job completed per unit of time) multiplied by the time working to find the amount of the job completed by each person. Two people working on the same job would be $R_1T_1 + R_2T_2 = 1$.

4. Write the equation to find how long it takes to complete the job when two people work together. They can complete the job by themselves in 4 hours and 5 hours respectfully.

a. $\frac{1}{4}x - \frac{1}{5}x = 1$

c. $\frac{1}{4}x + \frac{1}{5}x = 1$

d. $4x + 5x = 1$

b. $\frac{1}{9}x = 1$

5. John can complete the job in 6 hours, and Sue can complete the job in 4 hours. How long does it take them to complete the job when they work together?

a. $\frac{5}{12}$ hours

c. 2 hours

b. $\frac{12}{5}$ hours

d. $\frac{5}{2}$ hours

6. Jose can complete the job in a hours, and Maria can complete the job in b hours. How long does it take them to complete the job when they work together?

a. $a + b$ hours

c. $\frac{ab}{a+b}$ hours

b. $\frac{a+b}{ab}$ hours

d. $a - b$ hours

7. Al completed the job in 20 minutes. Al and Pam completed the job together in 12 minutes. How long does it take Pam to complete the job by herself?

a. 8 minutes

c. 32 minutes

b. 16 minutes

d. 30 minutes

Parent Tip: Percent mixture problems will use the following formula:
(amount of substance)(% of concentration) + (amount of substance)(% of concentration) =
(total amount of substance)(final % of concentration)

Choose the correct answer for the following.

8. How many ounces of a 12% salt solution must be added to 8 ounces of a 36% salt solution
    to obtain a 28% salt solution?

    a. $x(.12)+8(.36)=(x+8)(.28)$ c. $x(.28)+8(.36)=(x+8)(.12)$

    b. $x(.28)+8(.36)=(x+8)(.12)$ d. $x(.12)+8(.36)=8(.28)$

9. How many ounces of pure acid must be added to 10 liters of a 75% acid solution to obtain
    an 85% acid solution?

    a. $x(0)+10(.75)=(x+10)(.85)$ c. $x+10(.75)=10(.85)$

    b. $x+10(.75)=(x+10)(.85)$ d. $10(.75)=(x+10)(.85)$

10. How much water must be added to 6 ounces of a 20% acid solution to obtain a 15% acid
    solution?

    a.   5 ounces   c.   3 ounces

    b.   4 ounces   d.   2 ounces

Content Cluster: ALGEBRA - Sections 16 - 18

Objective: Students will understand the concepts of a relation and a function, determine whether a given relation defines a function and give pertinent information about given relations and functions.

Parent Tip: A relation is a set of ordered pairs.

Example: $\{(1,2),(1,3),(2,4)\}$

A function is a relation where every element in the domain is paired with exactly one element in the range. The domain is the set of all the first elements in a relation. The example has a domain of $\{1,2\}$. The range is the set of all the second elements in a relation. The example has a range of $\{2,3,4\}$. The mapping of the points is $1 \rightarrow 2, 1 \rightarrow 3, 2 \rightarrow 4$.

This is not a function (1 is mapped to 2 and 3).

Solve the following.

1. Write the relation

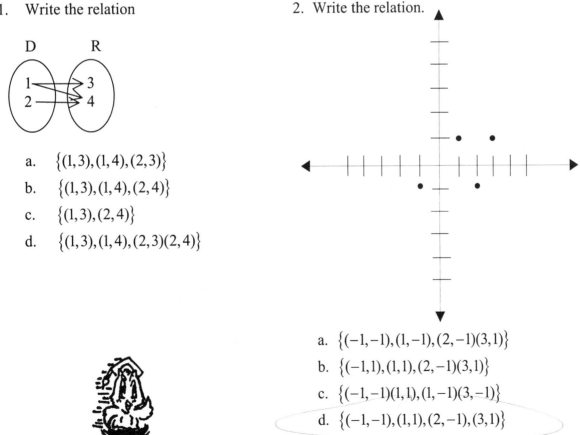

     a. $\{(1,3),(1,4),(2,3)\}$

     b. $\{(1,3),(1,4),(2,4)\}$

     c. $\{(1,3),(2,4)\}$

     d. $\{(1,3),(1,4),(2,3)(2,4)\}$

2. Write the relation.

     a. $\{(-1,-1),(1,-1),(2,-1)(3,1)\}$

     b. $\{(-1,1),(1,1),(2,-1)(3,1)\}$

     c. $\{(-1,-1)(1,1),(1,-1)(3,-1)\}$

     d. $\{(-1,-1),(1,1),(2,-1),(3,1)\}$

3. Each element of the domain of a function must map into how many elements in the range?

    a.   0
    b.   exactly one
    c.   two or more
    d.   one or more

4. Each of the range of a function must have been mapped from how many elements from the domain?

    a.   0
    b.   exactly one
    c.   two or more
    d.   one or more

Objective: Students will determine the domain of independent variables, and range of dependent variables defined by a graph, a set of ordered pairs, or symbolic expression.

Find the domain for questions 5 – 10.

5. $\{(1,2),(2,2),(3,3),(3,4)\}$

    a. $\{1,2,3\}$
    b. $\{2,3,4\}$
    c. $\{1,2,3,4\}$
    d. $\{1,2,3,3\}$

6.

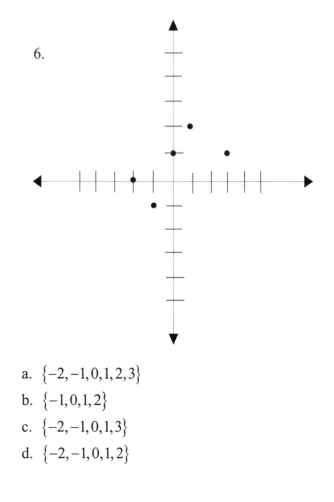

    a. $\{-2,-1,0,1,2,3\}$
    b. $\{-1,0,1,2\}$
    c. $\{-2,-1,0,1,3\}$
    d. $\{-2,-1,0,1,2\}$

7. $f(x) = x^2$

     a. $x \geq 0$
     b. $x \leq 0$
     c.   0
     d.   all real numbers

8. $g(x) = \sqrt{x}$

     a. $x \geq 0$
     b. $x \leq 0$
     c.   0
     d.   all real numbers

9. $f : x \rightarrow x + 2$, range $= \{0,1,2\}$

     a. $\{2,3,4\}$
     b. $\{-1,0,-1\}$
     c. $\{-2,-1,0\}$
     d. $\{0,1,2\}$

10. $g : x \rightarrow x^2 + 1$, range $= \{1,5\}$

     a. $\{-2,0,2\}$
     b. $\{-2,2\}$
     c. $\{1,2\}$
     d. $\{-2,0,1\}$

Find the range for questions 11 – 16.

11. $\{(-1,-1),(0,-1),(1,-1)\}$

     a. $\{-1,0,1\}$
     b. $\{-1\}$
     c. $\{-1,0\}$
     d. $\{-1,1\}$

12.

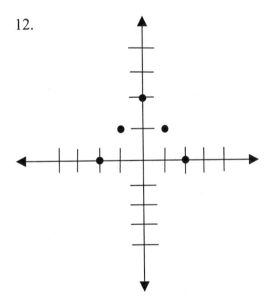

     a. $\{-1,0,1\}$
     b. $\{-2,-1,0,1,2\}$
     c. $\{1,2\}$
     d. $\{0,1,2\}$

13. $f(x) = 3x - 2$, domain $= \{-2, 1, 2\}$

    a. $\{1, 4\}$
    b. $\{-8, -1, 4\}$
    c. $\{-8, 1, 4\}$
    d. $\{-1, 1, 4\}$

14. $g(x) = -x^2 + 3$, domain $= \{-2, -1, 1\}$

    a. $\{7, 4\}$
    b. $\{-1, 1\}$
    c. $\{-1, 2\}$
    d. $\{-1, 2, 4\}$

15. $f : x \rightarrow x^2$

    a. $x \geq 0$
    b. $x \leq 0$
    c. 0
    d. all real numbers

16. $g : x \rightarrow -\sqrt{x}$

    a. $x \geq 0$
    b. $x \leq 0$
    c. 0
    d. all real numbers

Which of the following is <u>not</u> a function?

17.
a. 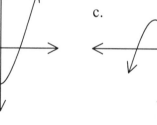 b. c. d.

18. a. $\{(-1, 3), (-1, 4), (-1, 5)\}$ b. $\{(2, 1), (3, 1), (4, 1)\}$

    c. $\{(1, 2), (2, 3), (3, 4)\}$ d. $\{(0, 1), (2, 3), (3, 1)\}$

19. a.   b.   c.   d.

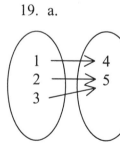 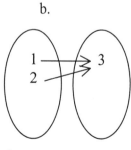 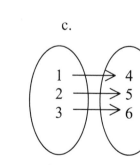 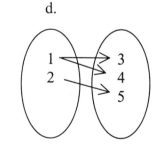

20. Why is the relation $\{(1, 2), (2, 3), (2, 4), (3, 5), (4, 5)\}$ not a function?

    a. 5 was mapped from 3 and 4.

    c. 2 was mapped to 3 and 4

    b. 3 and 4 was mapped to 5

    d. the relation is a function

Content Cluster: ALGEBRA - Section 19

Objective: Students will know the quadratic formula and are familiar with its proof by completing the square.

Parent Tip: Recall the process of completing the square with the polynomial $ax^2 + bx + c = 0$. The polynomial was transformed to $(x + \frac{b}{2a})^2 = \frac{b^2 - 4ac}{4a^2}$. Taking the square of both sides results in $x + \frac{b}{2a} = \frac{\pm\sqrt{b^2 - 4ac}}{2a}$. Solve for x. $x = \frac{-b \pm \sqrt{b^2 - 4ac}}{2a}$. This is known as the quadratic formula used for solving equations in the form $ax^2 + bx + c = 0$.

Choose the correct answer.

1. What must be added to both sides to complete the square for $x^2 - \frac{b}{a}x = -\frac{c}{a}$?

   a. $\dfrac{b^2}{a^2}$

   b. $\dfrac{b}{2a}$

   c. $\dfrac{b}{a}$

   d. $\dfrac{b^2}{4a^2}$

2. If $ax^2 + bx = -c$, what must you divide by next to complete the square?

   a. a
   b. b

   c. c
   d. $-c$

3. $\sqrt{\dfrac{b^2 - 4ac}{4a^2}}$ simplifies to _____.

   a. $\dfrac{b - 2\sqrt{ac}}{2a}$

   b. $\dfrac{\sqrt{b^2 - 4ac}}{2a}$

   c. $\dfrac{b - 2c}{2a}$

   d. $\dfrac{\sqrt{b^2 - 4ac}}{4a}$

4. Solve for x, $ax^2 + bx + c = 0$.

   a. $x = \dfrac{b \pm \sqrt{b^2 - 4ac}}{2a}$

   b. $x = \dfrac{-b \pm \sqrt{b^2 - 4ac}}{2a}$

   c. $x = \dfrac{-b \pm \sqrt{b^2 - 4ac}}{4a}$

   d. $x = \dfrac{-b + \sqrt{b^2 - 4ac}}{2a}$

Content Cluster: ALGEBRA - Section 20

Objective: Students will use the quadratic formula to find the roots of second degree polynomials and solve quadratic equations.

Parent Tip: Get the equation in the form $ax^2 + bx + c = 0$. Find a, b, c and replace the values in the quadratic formula to find the roots or solutions.

Solve each equation by using the quadratic formula.

1. $5x^2 - 3x - 1 = 0$

   a. $x = \dfrac{3 \pm \sqrt{29}}{10}$

   b. $x = \dfrac{-3 \pm \sqrt{29}}{10}$

   c. $x = \dfrac{3 \pm \sqrt{11}}{10}$

   d. $x = \dfrac{3 \pm \sqrt{-11}}{10}$

2. $2x^2 + 6x + 3 = 0$

   a. $x = \dfrac{-3 \pm \sqrt{12}}{4}$

   b. $x = -6 \pm \sqrt{3}$

   c. $x = \dfrac{-3 \pm \sqrt{3}}{2}$

   d. $x = -3 \pm \sqrt{3}$

3. $x^2 - 8x = -4$

   a. $x = 4 \pm 2\sqrt{5}$

   b. $x = 4 \pm 4\sqrt{3}$

   c. $x = -4 \pm 2\sqrt{3}$

   d. $x = 4 \pm 2\sqrt{3}$

4. $3x^2 = -5x + 4$

   a. $x = \dfrac{-5 \pm \sqrt{73}}{6}$

   b. $x = \dfrac{5 \pm \sqrt{73}}{6}$

   c. $x = \dfrac{-5 \pm \sqrt{23}}{6}$

   d. No Solution

5. $2x^2 + x - 3 = 0$

　　a.　　$x = \dfrac{-3}{2}, \dfrac{1}{2}$

　　b.　　$x = \dfrac{3}{2}, \dfrac{-1}{2}$

　　c.　　$x = \dfrac{-3}{2}, \dfrac{-1}{2}$

　　d.　　No Solution

6. $x^2 - 5x - 6 = 0$

　　a.　　$x = -6, 1$

　　b.　　$x = 6, -1$

　　c.　　$x = 2, 3$

　　d.　　$x = -2, -3$

7. $3x^2 - 4x - 2 = 0$

　　a.　　$x = \dfrac{2 \pm 2\sqrt{10}}{3}$

　　b.　　$x = \dfrac{-2 \pm 2\sqrt{10}}{3}$

　　c.　　$x = \dfrac{2 \pm \sqrt{10}}{3}$

　　d.　　$x = \dfrac{-2 \pm \sqrt{10}}{3}$

8. $x^2 + 6x - 1 = 0$

　　a.　　$x = 3 \pm \sqrt{10}$

　　b.　　$x = -3 \pm \sqrt{10}$

　　c.　　$x = 3 \pm 2\sqrt{10}$

　　d.　　$x = -3 \pm 2\sqrt{10}$

9. $2x^2 = 4x + 1$

　　a.　　$x = 1 \pm \sqrt{6}$

　　b.　　$x = 2 \pm \sqrt{3}$

　　c.　　$x = -1 \pm \sqrt{6}$

　　d.　　$x = \dfrac{2 \pm \sqrt{6}}{2}$

nt Cluster: ALGEBRA - Section 21

Objective: Students will graph quadratic functions and know their roots are the x-intercepts.

Parent Tip: The graph of a quadratic function $(y = ax^2 + bx + c)$ is a parabola.

$(a > 0)$ or $(a < 0)$

the vertex of the parabola can be found by finding the x-coordinate $(x = \dfrac{-b}{2a})$, and substitute the x value into the equation to find the y-coordinate.

Example: $y = -2x^2 + 8x - 5$

$$x = \frac{-8}{2(-2)} = 2. \quad y = -2(2)^2 + 8(2) - 5 \text{ or } y = 3. \text{ Vertex } (2,3).$$

Since a is negative, the graph goes down.

Choose the correct answer.

1. Graph $y = x^2 + 2x - 3$

   a.   b.   c.   d.

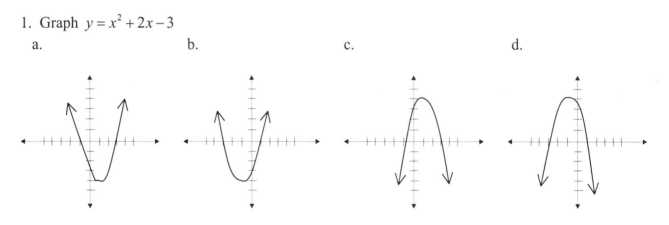

2. Graph $y = -x^2 + 2$

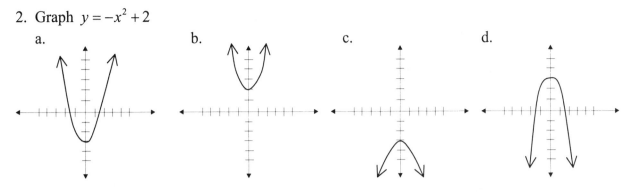

a.   b.   c.   d.

3. Find the vertex and determine if the graph goes up or down for $y = -3x^2 + 12x - 8$.

a.   b. (2,4)   c.   d. (-2,4)

(2,4)   (-2,4)

Parent Tip: The roots for $y = ax^2 + bx + c$ are the values for x when $y = 0$. From a graph, this will be the x-intercepts.

4. Find the roots for the graph $y = -x^2 - 2x + 3$. (use the graph)

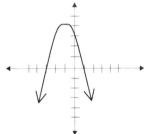

  a. $x = -3,1$ c. $x = 1,3$

  b. $x = -3,1,3$ d. $x = -3,-1$

5. Find the roots for the graph $y = x^2 - 4x$. (make a graph)

  a. $x = -4,4$ c. $x = 0,4$

  b. $x = -4,0$ d. $x = -4,0,4$

Content Cluster: ALGEBRA - Section 22

Objective: Students use the quadratic formula and/or factoring techniques to determine whether the graph of a quadratic function will intersect the x-axis in zero, one, or two points.

Parent Tip: The part of the quadratic formula contained inside the square root $(b^2 - 4ac)$ is called the discriminant. The value of $b^2 - 4ac$ will determine how many roots or the number of times the graph will intersect the x-axis. $b^2 - 4ac > 0$ 2 real solutions (2 points)

$$b^2 - 4ac = 0 \quad \text{1 real solution (1 point)}$$
$$b^2 - 4ac < 0 \quad \text{no real solutions (zero points)}$$

For questions 1 – 3, find how many times the graph will intersect the x-axis.

1. $y = 3x^2 - 5x + 4$

   a. 2 points
   b. 1 point
   c. zero points

2. $y = -x^2 + 4x - 4$

   a. 2 points
   b. 1 point
   c. zero points

3. $y = 2x^2 - 6x - 11$

   a. 2 points
   b. 1 point
   c. zero points

For questions 4 – 6, find how many real solutions to each equation.

4. $4x^2 - 20x + 25 = 0$

   a. 2 real solutions
   b. 1 real solution
   c. no real solutions

5. $-3x^2 + 6x - 4 = 0$

   a. 2 real solutions
   b. 1 real solution
   c. no real solutions

6. $5x^2 - 2x - 1 = 0$

   a. 2 real solutions
   b. 1 real solution
   c. no real solutions

Parent Tip: To find the number of times the graph will intersect the x-axis by factoring, let $y = 0$ and solve for the number of roots. 2 roots $\rightarrow$ 2 points. 1 double root $\rightarrow$ 1 point. You must find the value of the discriminant to show zero points.

For questions 7 – 9, factor or find the discriminant to determine how many times the graph will intersect the x-axis.

7. $y = x^2 + 6x + 5$

   a. 2 points
   b. 1 point
   c. zero points

8. $y = x^2 - 6x + 9$

   a. 2 points
   b. 1 point
   c. zero points

9. $y = x^2 + 2x + 4$

   a. 2 points
   b. 1 point
   c. zero points

Content Cluster: ALGEBRA - Section 23

Objective: Students will apply quadratic equations to physical problems such as motion of an object under the force of gravity.

Parent Tip: These problems involve a formula. Substitute the values, and solve for the quadratic equation. Following are the three formulas involving gravity.

1. $h = vt - \frac{1}{2}gt^2$ used when an object is shot in the air. h = height (feet), v = velocity $(\frac{ft}{sec})$, g = gravity $(32\frac{ft}{sec^2})$, t = time (sec). Putting in the gravity value, this formula can be written as $h = vt - 16t^2$.

2. $s = vt + \frac{1}{2}gt^2$ used for an object falling with an initial velocity. s = distance fallen (feet), the $v, g,$ and t are the same as above. This formula can be written as $s = vt + 16t^2$.

3. $s = \frac{1}{2}gt^2$ used for an object that is dropped with no initial velocity. The variables are the same as previously stated. This formula can be written as $s = 16t^2$.

For questions 1 and 2, use $h = vt - 16t^2$.

1. An object is shot into the air with a velocity of $64\frac{ft}{sec}$. When will it be 60 feet high?

   a. 2 seconds

   b. 2 and $\frac{5}{2}$ seconds

   c. 1 and $\frac{3}{2}$ seconds

   d. $\frac{3}{2}$ and $\frac{5}{2}$ seconds

2. An object is shot into the air with a velocity of $160\frac{ft}{sec}$. When will it be 256 feet high?

   a. 2 and 12 seconds

   b. 2 and 8 seconds

   c. 4 and 8 seconds

   d. 2 and 4 seconds

For questions 3 and 4, use $s = vt + 16t^2$.

3. An object is thrown down with an initial velocity of $16\dfrac{ft}{sec}$. When will the object have fallen 320 feet?

    a. 4 seconds
    b. 5 seconds

    c. 2 seconds
    d. 10 seconds

4. An object is thrown down with an initial velocity of $8\dfrac{ft}{sec}$. When will the object have fallen 120 feet?

    a. 2 seconds

    b. 3 seconds

    c. $\dfrac{3}{2}$ seconds

    d. $\dfrac{5}{2}$ seconds

For questions 5 and 6, use $s = 16t^2$.

5. An object is dropped from a cliff that is 1600 feet high. When will the object hit the ground?

    a. 100 seconds
    b. $\sqrt{10}$ seconds

    c. 10 seconds
    d. ± 10 seconds

6. An object is dropped from a cliff that is 192 feet high. When will the object hit the ground?

    a. $2\sqrt{6}$ seconds
    b. 4 seconds

    c. $2\sqrt{3}$ seconds
    d. $3\sqrt{2}$ seconds

Content Cluster: ALGEBRA - Section 24

Objective: Students will use and know simple aspects of a logical argument. Students will explain the difference between inductive and deductive reasoning and identify and provide examples of each.

> **Parent Tip:** Inductive reasoning is based on past observations or patterns. Deductive reasoning is based on accepted facts such as axioms, theorems, or definitions.

Choose the correct answer.

1. Which of the following is based on deductive reasoning?

   a. A man observes trash in the street and concludes, this is a dirty town.
   b. A man falls and thinks he may have broken a bone.
   c. A doctor looks at the x-ray and finds a broken bone.
   d. A boy notices it is cold and concludes, it is always cold on this day.

2. Which of the following is based on inductive reasoning?

   a. Sally discovers $a + b = b + a$ for the numbers tried.
   b. John knows the commutative property is a fact that $a + b = b + a$.
   c. Alex uses a theorem to prove his argument.
   d. Betty recites a definition to prove her conclusion.

3. Use inductive reasoning to find the next number in the sequence. 2, 4, 6, 8, 10, ___

   a. 8
   b. 11
   c. 9
   d. 12

4. Use inductive reasoning to find the next number in the sequence. 1, 1, 2, 3, 5, 8, 13, ____

   a. 21
   b. 20
   c. 22
   d. 19

Objective: Students will identify the hypothesis and conclusion in logical deduction.

Parent Tip: If p, then q. p is the hypothesis, and q is the conclusion. Not all statements are written in the if-then form. Other ways are: q, if p; p implies q; or p only if q.

Choose the correct answer.

If it rains, then I will get wet.

5.   It rains is the _____ .

   a.   hypothesis
   b.   conclusion

6.   I will get wet is the _____ .

   a.   hypothesis
   b.   conclusion

I will study, if you help me.

7.   I will study is the _____ .

   a.   hypothesis
   b.   conclusion

8.   You help me is the _____ .

   a.   hypothesis
   b.   conclusion

Objective: Students will use counterexamples to show that an assertion is false and recognize that a single counterexample is sufficient to refuse an assertion.

Parent Tip: To show a statement is false, find a true hypothesis and a false conclusion.

Example: If $xy > 0$, then $x > 0$

Let $x = -2$ and $y = -3$. When you substitute: If 6>0, then –2>0. True – hypothesis, False – conclusion. False statement.

Find the answer to show each statement is false.

9. If a number is divisible by 4, then it is divisible by 6.

   a. 24
   b. 6
   c. 8
   d. 12

10. If $xy < 0$, then $y < 0$.

   a. $x = 4, y = 1$
   b. $x = 4, y = -1$
   c. $x = -4, y = -1$
   d. $x = -4, y = 1$

11. If $x^2 = 2x$, then $x = 2$.

   a. $x = 2$
   b. $x = 0$
   c. $x = -2$
   d. $x = 1$

12. If $a = b$, then $\dfrac{a}{c} = \dfrac{b}{c}$ for all values for c.

   a. $c = 0$
   b. $c = 5$
   c. $c = -1$
   d. $c = 100$

Content Cluster: ALGEBRA - Section 25

Objective: Students will use properties of the number system to judge the validity of results, to justify each step of a procedure and to prove or disprove statements.

> **Parent Tip:** Knowledge of the language in mathematics is essential. Flash cards can be helpful.

Use the following to answer questions 1 – 3.

Statements	Reasons
1. $x + 3 = 7$	1.
2. $x + 3 + -3 = 7 + -3$	2.
3. $x + 0 = 4$	3.
4. $x = 4$	4.

1. Why is statement 2 valid from statement 1?

     a. Subtraction Property
     b. Addition Property
     c. Identity Property
     d. Additive Inverse Property

2. How did $x + 3 + -3$ in statement 2 change to $x + 0$ in statement 3?

     a. Subtraction Property
     b. Addition Property
     c. Identity Property
     d. Additive Inverse Property

3. How did $x + 0$ in statement 3 change to x in statement 4?

     a. Subtraction Property
     b. Addition Property
     c. Identity Property
     d. Additive Inverse Property

Objective: Students will use properties of numbers to construct valid arguments for, or formulate counterexamples to, claimed assertions.

4. Which of the following is **not** a valid property?

   a. $a+b=b+a$
   b. $ab=ba$
   c. $a-b=b-a$
   d. If $a=b$, then $b=a$

5. What number shows $x^2 = x+x$ is **not** a valid property?

   a. 1
   b. 0
   c. 2
   d. $x^2 = x+x$ is a valid property

6. Which of the following is **not** an example of the Distributive Property?

   a. $a(b+c) = ab+ac$
   b. $-(x+y) = -x + -y$
   c. $3(x+2y) = 3x+6y$
   d. $3(x+y) = (x+y)(3)$

Objective: Students will judge the validity of an argument based on whether the properties of the real number system and order of operations have been applied correctly at each step.

7. Which of the following is **not** a correct step?

   a. $3+(5-2) = 3+3$
   b. $4+5\cdot2 = 9\cdot2$
   c. $-2(x+y) = -2(y+x)$
   d. $5x+0 = 5x$

8. Which of the following is **not** a correct step?

   a. $7-3+2 = 7-5$
   b. $8 \div 4 \cdot 2 = 2 \cdot 2$
   c. $5-3^2 = 5-9$
   d. $4^2 - 1^2 = 16-1$

9.   Which of the following is **not** a correct step?

   a. $-3(x-y) = -3x + 3y$
   b. $-(-x-y) = x + y$
   c. $2(x+3y) + x = 2x + 6y + x$
   d. $-2(3x + 4y - 1) = -6x - 8y - 2$

Objective: Students will determine if a statement is true sometimes, always, or never given a specific algebraic statement involving linear, quadratic, or absolute value expressions, equations or inequalities.

Parent Tip: If students substitute values to show if the statement is true, and try to find values to show the statement is false. Try zero, positive numbers, and negative numbers. Recall properties are always true.

Determine if the following statements are true sometimes, always, or never. Each value can represent any real number.

10. $|x| = x$

   a.   sometimes
   b.   always
   c.   never

11. $x^2 + x = x(x+1)$

   a.   sometimes
   b.   always
   c.   never

12. $x^2 < 0$

   a.   sometimes
   b.   always
   c.   never

13. $a(b+c) = ab + ac$

   a.   sometimes
   b.   always
   c.   never

14. $x = \dfrac{-1}{x}$

   a.   sometimes
   b.   always
   c.   never

15. $x^2 = x + x$

   a.   sometimes
   b.   always
   c.   never

MATH
Answer Key

ALGEBRA

Section 1
1. d
2. c
3. a
4. a
5. c
6. d
7. b
8. a
9. a
10. d

Section 2
1. b
2. a
3. b
4. d
5. a
6. c
7. b
8. a
9. c
10. d
11. a
12. b
13. c
14. c
15. a
16. b
17. d
18. a
19. c
20. b

Section 3
1. c
2. b
3. a
4. b
5. d
6. b

7. c
8. a
9. c
10. d

Section 4
1. c
2. b
3. d
4. b
5. a
6. c
7. d
8. a
9. b
10. a
11. c
12. c

Section 5
1. d
2. c
3. a
4. d
5. b
6. c
7. d
8. b
9. d
10. a
11. b
12. c

Section 6
1. c
2. a
3. c
4. b
5. d
6. a
7. b
8. b

9. d
10. c

Section 7
1. b
2. d
3. a
4. d
5. c
6. c
7. b
8. a

Section 8
1. b
2. c
3. a
4. b
5. a
6. a
7. c
8. c
9. a
10. d

Section 9
1. d
2. b
3. c
4. b
5. a
6. c
7. a
8. c

Section 10
1. d
2. c
3. a
4. d
5. b
6. d

7. c
8. a
9. a
10. b
11. d
12. c

Section 11
1. d
2. b
3. a
4. d
5. c
6. b
7. d
8. c
9. a
10. b
11. a
12. d
13. c

Section 12
1. b
2. d
3. a
4. b
5. b
6. c

Section 13
1. b
2. d
3. a
4. d
5. b
6. c
7. a
8. c

Section 14
1. a
2. b
3. c
4. b
5. d
6. c
7. c
8. d
9. b
10. c
11. a
12. d
13. a
14. c
15. d

Section 15
1. c
2. d
3. a
4. c
5. b
6. c
7. d
8. a
9. b
10. d

Sections 16 – 18
1. b
2. d
3. b
4. d
5. a
6. c
7. d
8. a
9. c
10. a
11. b
12. d
13. c
14. c
15. a
16. b
17. d
18. a
19. d
20. c

Section 19
1. d
2. a
3. b
4. b

Section 20
1. a
2. c
3. d
4. a
5. d
6. b
7. c
8. b
9. d

Section 21
1. b
2. d
3. b
4. a
5. c

Section 22
1. c
2. b
3. a
4. b
5. c
6. a
7. a
8. b
9. c

Section 23
1. d
2. b
3. a
4. d
5. c

6. c

Section 24
1. c
2. a
3. d
4. a
5. a
6. b
7. b
8. a
9. c
10. d
11. b
12. a

Section 25
1. b
2. d
3. c
4. c
5. a
6. d
7. b
8. a
9. d
10. a
11. b
12. c
13. b
14. c
15. a

SOCIAL SCIENCE
U.S. HISTORY AND GEOGRAPHY

Content Cluster: EVENTS PRECEDING THE FOUNDING OF
THE NATION

Objectives: To evaluate the student's knowledge of: (1) the relationship between the moral and political ideas of the Great Awakening and the development of revolutionary fervor, (2) the philosophy of government expressed in the Declaration of Independence, (3) how the American Revolution affected other nations, and (4) the nation's blend of philosophical principles and English parliamentary traditions.

Parent Tip: This cluster focuses on the major events that preceded the founding of our nation. While many of these events will be familiar to your child from previous years' study, in the eighth grade she will analyze the ideas, events, and issues with greater sophistication. To assist your child, encourage her to reason beyond the dates and facts of "who" and "what" questions; formulate questions that ask "why" and discuss the responses with her. For example, while it is important to know the names of the members of the committee that drafted the Declaration of Independence, it is equally important to understand why each member was chosen for the task.

Engage your child in conversations about historical and political issues. Focus on the political and religious traditions that influenced our democratic institutions and the framing of the Constitution. The following exercises can serve to guide you through many discussions. Talk with your child about why she chose a particular answer to a question, and why the other responses to the question were improper choices.

Choose the best answer.

1. The Great Awakening of the 1740s

    a. refers to an excitement about religion that swept through the colonies.
    b. emphasized the importance of having sincere religious feelings.
    c. was a force for religious toleration.
    d. all of the above.

2. The Great Awakening had important political consequences in encouraging democratic ideals because

   a. the Judeo-Christian heritage of most colonists stressed that people were equal in the eyes of God.
   b. the Judeo-Christian heritage of most colonists encouraged an allegiance to God, which implied that the power of the state was not absolute.
   c. people experienced a freedom of choice in their religious lives that they wanted in their political lives.
   d. all of the above.

3. The Enlightenment refers to

   a. the invention of electrical appliances.
   b. a philosophy that rejected the power of reason and scientific study.
   c. a belief that human reason and careful study will prevail in an orderly universe.
   d. the ideas of college educated colonists.

4. The Declaration of Independence

   a. rejected the ideas of the Enlightenment philosophers.
   b. was written mainly by Thomas Jefferson, who was part of a committee that included John Adams, Roger Sherman, Benjamin Franklin, and Robert Livingston.
   c. preceded any fighting with the British soldiers in America.
   d. begins with a declaration of war on England without stating any reasons .

5. The Preamble of the Declaration of Independence

   a. begins, "When in the course of human events, it becomes necessary for one people to dissolve the political bands which have connected them with another."
   b. makes no reference to the laws of nature or God.
   c. refers to King George III and slave trade.
   d. declares war on the British monarchy.

6. The Declaration of Rights section of the Declaration of Independence

   a. begins, "We hold these truths to be self-evident, that all men are created equal."
   b. begins, "When in the course of human events, it becomes necessary for one people to dissolve the political bands which have connected them with another."
   c. begins, "The history of the present King of Great Britain is a history of repeated injuries and usurpations."
   d. begins, "For the support of this Declaration, with a firm reliance on the protection of divine Providence, we mutually pledge to each other our Lives, our Fortunes and our sacred Honor."

7. Among the truths that the drafters considered to be self-evident or obvious, were that

    a. all men are created equal before the law.
    b. people have God-given rights that no just government can take away for any reason.
    c. life, liberty, and the pursuit of happiness are rights with which all men are born.
    d. all of the above

8. The term *absolute despotism* means

    a. rule by an unkind king.
    b. chaotic anarchy.
    c. rule with unlimited power.
    d. unquestioned democratic ideals.

9. According to the Declaration, what is the right and duty of a people who suffer at the hands of an absolute despot?

    a. vote him out of office
    b. overthrow the government and change the system
    c. petition the queen
    d. peacefully write a Declaration of Independence

10. The philosophy of government expressed in the Declaration can be summarized as

    a. the best government is one that governs from American soil.
    b. in a democracy, the power to rule comes from the people who are to be governed, and that power must be used to benefit them.
    c. the right to rule the people in a country passes from God to the ruling monarch.
    d. the enlightened common man must be in control of his own life.

11. Which of the following <u>cannot</u> fairly be said about the American Revolution?

    a. It inspired the French Revolution.
    b. It weakened Great Britain in its European rivalry with France.
    c. It did little to benefit the Native Americans.
    d. It had no effect on other nations because America was geographically isolated.

12. Which of the following does <u>not</u> describe the new nation?

    a. It mirrored the English system of government.
    b. It embraced republicanism, with its power resting with representatives elected by the people.
    c. It adopted concepts contained in the Magna Carta.
    d. It created Congress in the image of English parliamentary traditions.

Content Cluster: POLITICAL PRINCIPLES UNDERLYING THE U.S. CONSTITUTION

Objectives: To evaluate the student's understanding of (1) significant historical political documents; (2) the Articles of Confederation and the Constitution; (3) the major debates that occurred during the development of the Constitution; (4) the role of significant political leaders in the writing and ratification of the Constitution; (6) the Bill of Rights; and (7) the principles of federalism, dual sovereignty, separation of powers, and checks and balances.

Parent Tip: Children understand history in a meaningful way when they are able to make connections between the past and their own lives. This cluster, which focuses on the U.S. Constitution, provides opportunities for rich discussions about individual rights, as they existed in the past and now, in our country and in other nations.

Choose the best answer.

1. The _____ provided the basis for establishing parliamentary government, addressed the rights of ordinary people, and guaranteed a trial by a jury of one's peers.

    a. English Bill of Rights
    b. Charter of the Great Council
    c. Magna Carta
    d. Mayflower Compact

2. The _____ declared that the monarch could not impose any tax, establish or abolish any law, or maintain a peacetime army without Parliament's consent.

    a. English Bill of Rights
    b. Charter of the Great Council
    c. Magna Carta
    d. Mayflower Compact

3. The _____ represents the first known conscious decision of a people to create a government where none had existed before.

    a. English Bill of Rights
    b. Charter of the Great Council
    c. Magna Carta
    d. Mayflower Compact

4. The Articles of Confederation

    a. provided a skeletal framework for the U.S. Constitution.
    b. abolished the "league of friendship" that existed among the colonies.
    c. provided for a chief executive who could regulate interstate commerce.
    d. included both a central and state government to represent the people.

Exercises 5 - 24 refer to the Articles of Confederation and the U.S. Constitution. Determine whether each phrase is true with respect to—or was a provision of—either, both, or neither document. Select the best answer from the following choices:

    a. **Articles of Confederation**
    b. **U. S. Constitution**
    c. **both documents**
    d. **neither document**

5. no national chief executive

6. national system of courts

7. power to levy taxes for the nation

8. power of states to print money and make coins

9. weak central government

10. powerful central government

11. governors chosen by the Crown

12. legislators appointed

13. power to regulate interstate commerce

14. power to enforce treaties

15. provision for state governments

16. lack of a uniform currency

17. amendment only by unanimous approval of the states

18. unicameral legislature

19. bicameral legislature

20. drafted in 1777

21. permanent national Congress

22. legislative, executive, and judicial branch

23. power to pass laws

24. power to enforce laws

Choose the best answer.

25. Which document begins, "We the People of the United States, in Order to form a more perfect Union, establish Justice, insure domestic Tranquility, provide for the common defense, promote the general Welfare, and secure the Blessings of Liberty to ourselves and our Posterity . . . ?"

   a. the Declaration of Independence
   b. the Articles of Confederation
   c. the Constitution of the United States
   d. the Treaty of Paris

26. Which of the following is <u>not</u> an accurate statement about the Constitutional Convention?

   a. George Washington, Benjamin Franklin, James Madison, Roger Sherman, Gouverneur Morris, and Alexander Hamilton attended the Convention.
   b. The members adhered to a strict rule of secrecy.
   c. It was held in Washington, D.C.
   d. Within the first five days, the delegates decided to abandon the Articles of Confederation and draft a new document.

27. Which of the following was <u>not</u> the subject of significant debate at the Convention?

   a. the election of the president of the Convention
   b. reconciling the power of local control in the states with the power of the new central government
   c. the extent to which the functions and powers of the national and state governments should be defined
   d. the number, nature, and of the branches of government

28. The Virginia Plan

    a. called for a central federal government with a bicameral legislature, an executive branch, and a judicial branch.
    b. proposed that the citizens would elect the legislature, but the legislature would elect the executive.
    c. was opposed by the smaller states' delegates because it specified that representation in the legislature would be proportionate to state population.
    d. all of the above

29. The New Jersey Plan

    a. suggested keeping most of the Articles of Confederation intact.
    b. gave all states equal representation in the legislature.
    c. proposed a separate, independent Supreme Court.
    d. all of the above

30. As proposed by Roger Sherman, the Connecticut Compromise (Great Compromise),

    a. was actually no compromise at all.
    b. provided for a bicameral legislature with equal representation for the states in one house and representation based on population in the other.
    c. rejected the notion of the Electoral College to elect the chief executive.
    d. all of the above

31. Regarding the disputes about slavery,

    a. the southern delegates would not grant freed blacks the vote, but wanted slaves counted for the purpose of representation in the legislature.
    b. under the Three-Fifths Compromise, for purposes of levying taxes and apportioning representatives, a slave was counted as three-fifths of a person.
    c. although they addressed the issue, the framers avoided using the word *slavery* anywhere in the Constitution.
    d. all of the above

32. The Delegates to the Convention tried to prevent the misuse of power through a system of

    a. restraint of trade
    b. appointed officials
    c. checks and balances
    d. ratification

33. A system in which the state and national governments share power is called

    a. federalism.
    b. states' rights.
    c. republicanism.
    d. checks and balances.

34. _____ powers are given to the national government, while _____powers are held by the states.

    a. General/specific
    b. Reserved / shared
    c. Establishment / unimportant
    d. Delegated / reserved

For each of the powers referenced in exercises 35 - 50, determine whether the power is one that is held by the national government, the state government, or one that is shared by both. Select the best answer from the following choices:

    a. power delegated to the national government
    b. power belonging to the state governments
    c. power shared by the national and state governments

35. coin money

36. regulate interstate commerce and foreign trade

37. establish and maintain schools

38. establish post offices

39. establish foreign policy

40. levy taxes

41. establish courts

42. maintain law and order

43. maintain armed forces and declare war

44. charter banks

45. borrow money

46. provide for public safety

47. make marriage laws, corporation laws, and laws regulating business within the state

48. provide for public welfare

49. make all laws necessary and proper for carrying out delegated powers

50. assume all powers not delegated to the national government or prohibited to the states

Choose the best answer.

51. The supporters of the Constitution called themselves _____, while those who opposed its ratification were called _____.

    a. Liberals / Conservatives
    b. Radicals / Loyalists
    c. Ratificationists / Confederates
    d. Federalists / Antifederalists

52. In defense of the Constitution, Alexander Hamilton, John Jay, and James Madison wrote a series of 85 newspaper letters known as the _____.

    a. *Bill of Rights*
    b. *Unalienable Rights*
    c. *Federalist Papers*
    d. *Antifederalist Papers*

53. The Antifederalists

    a. were concerned about the possibility of a too powerful chief executive being elected at the expense of individual liberties.
    b. included Revolutionary leaders and supporters of states' rights, such as Patrick Henry of Virginia and Governor George Clinton of New York.
    c. were eventually persuaded to support ratification after they were promised that a bill of individuals' rights would be added to the Constitution.
    d. all of the above

54. The First Amendment protects

    a. freedom of religion, freedom of speech, freedom of the press.
    b. the right to assemble peacefully and to petition grievances to the government.
    c. all of the above
    d. none of the above

55. The Fourth Amendment

    a. protects the people's right to bear arms.
    b. protects the right to privacy and forbids unlawful searches and seizures.
    c. prohibits cruel and unusual punishment.
    d. prohibits the quartering of troops.

56. The Fifth Amendment

    a. guarantees that no one may be deprived of life, liberty, or property without due process of law
    b. requires separation of church and state
    c. requires a defendant to testify against himself.
    d. both choice *a* and choice *c*

57. Which of the following provisions is <u>not</u> included in the Bill of Rights?

    a. powers reserved to the states
    b. powers reserved to the people
    c. protection of people's rights against violation by the state governments
    d. right to a speedy, fail trial

58. Which of the following provisions is <u>not</u> included in the Articles of the Constitution?

    a. establishment of the legislative, executive, and judicial branches of government
    b. establishment of the President's cabinet
    c. amendment process
    d. supremacy of national law

59. Regarding the issue of religion in the new nation, which of the following is <u>not</u> true?

    a. The founding fathers were in agreement that the church should not receive any money or support from the government.
    b. Patrick Henry felt strongly that the government should give tax money to the churches to encourage piety and good morals.
    c. Thomas Jefferson and James Madison led the effort to abolish taxes that were reserved to go to churches.
    d. Jefferson helped pass a law in Virginia declaring that the government could not interfere in church affairs or matters of conscience.

60. Which of the following is not a part of the system of checks and balances?

    a. Presidential approval or veto of federal bills.
    b. Congressional override of veto.
    c. Supreme Court ruling that a law is unconstitutional.
    d. Establishment of banking laws

Content Cluster: AMERICA'S POLITICAL SYSTEM AT WORK

Objectives: To evaluate the student's understanding of: (1) the early development of American political institutions and ideas, (2) the emergence of two political parties, (3) domestic resistance movements, (4) the basic law-making process, and (5) the functions and responsibilities of a free press.

Parent Tip: This cluster focuses on the development of our political system and the ways that our citizens' participation has shaped that system. It is noteworthy that one of the topics that the state has included in this cluster of standards is the "function and responsibilities of a free press." Engage your child in discussions about the role and influence of the media in the lives of Americans today. In what ways is the political process influenced by the modern media, and vice versa? How different are today's local elections from those of the 1800s? What about our national elections? Have the functions and responsibilities of the press changed over the course of the last 200 years?

Choose the best answer.

1. Between 1777 and 1781, the state constitutions codified various political ideas and institutions, including

    a. powerful governors who could control the legislatures.
    b. complete political equality to all residents.
    c. powerful state legislatures with elected representatives.
    d. government officials who were public masters, not public servants.

2. The Land Ordinances of 1785 and 1787 were great accomplishments of Congress under the Articles of Confederation because they

    a. were the first national stand against slavery.
    b. helped individuals to acquire frontier land as their private property, and they simultaneously funded public education.
    c. ensured that the frontier regions would never be mere American colonies, but equal states as their populations grew.
    d. all of the above

3. Article I of the Constitution gives _____ the power "to regulate Commerce with foreign Nations, and among the several states." This provision is generally referred to as the "_____."

    a. the President / commerce clause
    b. the governors / free trade clause
    c. the Congress / commerce clause
    d. the state legislatures / common market clause

4. Article I, Section 8, the Constitution's "elastic clause", or "_____ clause" gives _____ the power to make all laws that are needed in order to carry out the federal government's duties. This expressed power provides the constitutional basis for _____ powers.

    a. necessary and proper / Congress / implied
    b. mush pot / Congress / general
    c. sewing / the President / specific
    d. commerce / Supreme Court / judicial

5. The "_____ clause" of Article IV requires each state to honor the laws, records, and court decisions of other states, so a person cannot escape a legal obligation by moving from one state to another.

    a. fugitive
    b. full faith and credit
    c. legal obligations
    d. deadbeat

6. Which of the following was not a reason that the framers of the Constitution provided for a strong national government that could regulate trade, interstate commerce, and uniform coinage?

    a. After the Revolution, as far as commerce was concerned, each state treated the others as foreign nations.
    b. Under the Articles of Confederation, no one imposed any tariffs on imports or exports.
    c. Each state tried to keep money from going outside its own borders into other states, and to build up its own businesses and wealth at the expense of its neighbors.
    d. Each state issued its own money, and the people lost confidence in its value.

7. Thomas Jefferson and Alexander Hamilton agreed about which of the following?

    a. ratification of the Constitution--with both of them arguing in support of it
    b. foreign affairs--with both of them favoring neutrality in the French-English war
    c. economic issues--with both of them favoring farming over the growth of industry
    d. financial and banking issue--with both of them agreeing that Congress had the power to establish a national bank.

8. The disagreements between Jefferson and Hamilton formed the foundation of the two-party political system,

    a.   with each party generally defined and distinguished by its view of the nature of the federal government.

    b.   with Hamilton's Federalist party favoring a relatively powerful and active central government.

    c.   with Jefferson's Democratic-Republican party favoring a restrained central government, with the states and individuals having more power.

    d.   all of the above

9. Shays' Rebellion

    a.   can be attributed to the disparity in economic and class standing that existed between working-class frontier farmers, city workers, and small merchants on the one hand, and the large landowners, slaveholders, and international merchants of the city on the other hand.

    b.   caused Massachusetts to pass the Riot Act, which allowed the authorities to jail anyone without a trial.

    c.   was overcome by an army paid for by Boston's merchants, because the militia sided with the rebelling debtor farmers.

    d.   all of the above

10. The Whiskey Rebellion

    a.   was a revolt of Western Pennsylvania's corn farmers brought to overturn a high excise tax placed on whiskey.

    b.   was an uprising of the frontiersmen who wanted to drink free whiskey.

    c.   was the result of Jefferson's idea to tax whiskey in order to make money for the new government.

    d.   was the result of the government's prohibition on the sale of whiskey to soldiers.

11. A bill becomes a federal law

    a.   only after the secret ballots are tallied.

    b.   only after it is approved by both houses and the President signs it into law.

    c.   only if the President uses his veto power.

    d.   all of the above

12. Citizens can participate in the political process by

    a.   assisting with elections at the polls.

    b.   registering to vote and by voting in local, state, and national elections.

    c.   joining a political party and attending political functions.

    d.   all of the above.

13. The Alien and Sedition Acts posed a serious threat to First Amendment guarantees because they

    a.   gave the President the power to deport any alien he thought was dangerous.
    b.   prohibited assembly with intent to oppose any measure of the government.
    c.   forbade printing, uttering, or publishing anything false, scandalous, and malicious against the government.
    d.   all of the above

14. The functions and responsibilities of a free press include

    a.   prohibiting the government from suppressing embarrassing information.
    b.   encouraging open debate and discussion of public issues.
    c.   keeping people informed about issues that affect them.
    d.   all of the above.

Content Cluster: IDEALS OF THE NEW NATION

Objectives: To evaluate the student's understanding of: (1) the aspirations and ideals of the people of the new nation, (2) the policy significance of famous American speeches of the period, (3) the rise of capitalism, and (4) daily life in America.

> **Parent Tip:** This cluster focuses on the physical expansion and cultural growth of our nation under the administrations of George Washington, John Adams, Thomas Jefferson, James Madison, James Monroe, and John Quincy Adams, during the years 1787 – 1828. Read with your child various accounts of life in the early days of the nation, turning to American writers of the early nineteenth century such as James Fenimore Cooper, Washington Irving, and Henry Wadsworth Longfellow. The journals of explorers James Meriwether Lewis and William Clark provide an extraordinary account of their expedition through the frontier in 1804.

Choose the best answer.

1. In his Farewell Address of 1797, George Washington advised his countrymen to

    a. avoid foreign entanglements.
    b. preserve the financial credit of the country.
    c. beware of the danger that political parties might fragment the nation.
    d. all of the above

2. In his Inaugural Address of 1801, Thomas Jefferson

    a. reminded the nation that in the grand scheme of things, the two political parties had the same core of beliefs, republicanism and federalism.
    b. stated that his foreign policy would be to form a close alliance with France
    c. told the audience that the rights of minorities have precedence over majority rule.
    d. all of the above

3. Jefferson's Louisiana Purchase

    a. almost doubled the size of the United States at a cost of four cents an acre.
    b. gave America control of the port of New Orleans and the Mississippi River.
    c. removed the French threat from the frontier.
    d. all of the above

4. In an effort to stop the expansion onto their lands, a Shawnee holy man named the Prophet and his brother, _____, tried to unite Native Americans from the Great Lakes to the Gulf of Mexico, but they were overcome at _____ by General William Henry _____.

     a. Charbonneau / Fort Mandan / Clark
     b. Little Turtle / the Battle of Fallen Timbers / Gold
     c. Chief Tecumseh / Tippecanoe / Harrison
     d. Powhattan / Jamestown / Jackson

5. At the time of the Lewis and Clark expedition, Spain

     a. owned Spanish Florida, the land south of Georgia and the Mississippi Territory, and east of the Mississippi River.
     b. owned the land west of the Louisiana Purchase from the Rocky Mountains to the Pacific Ocean, including Mexico and the land north to the Oregon Territory.
     c. was in an alliance with England, which ruled Canada.
     d. all of the above

6. In the Transcontinental Treaty of 1819,

     a. France took back part of Louisiana, including New Orleans.
     b. Spain retained Texas for itself, but ceded Florida and the land north of Texas (extending to the Pacific Ocean) to the United States.
     c. Great Britain ceded Canada and the Oregon Territory to the United States.
     d. Russia, Great Britain, and Spain ceded the Oregon Country to the United States.

7. James Monroe's years as President are referred to as the "Era of Good Feelings" because

     a. the Northeast economy expanded rapidly, with manufacturing bringing prosperity to the region.
     b. American was beginning to participate in the Industrial Revolution.
     c. there was little chance that the United States would engage in another war with Britain.
     d. all of the above

8. During the 1800s the United States began the change from a(n) _____ to a(n) _____ nation.

     a. rural / urban
     b. urban / rural
     c. industrial / diverse
     d. mechanical / agrarian

9. Although he was a Democratic-Republican, President Monroe broke with
    _____ and supported the _____, a decision that pleased the Northeast
    and angered Westerners.

    a. Alexander Hamilton / abolitionists
    b. Thomas Jefferson / rechartering of the Bank of the United States
    c. Alexander Hamilton / Monroe Doctrine
    d. supporters of commerce / farmers

10. President Monroe favored _____, high taxes placed on foreign goods to
    make the cost of American goods more competitive.

    a. tithes
    b. inflation
    c. protective tariffs
    d. credit terms

11. The poetry of Henry Wadsworth Longfellow includes

    a. "Hiawatha."
    b. "Paul Revere's Ride."
    c. "The Courtship of Miles Standish."
    d. all of the above

12. James Fenimore Cooper wrote

    a. *The Deerslayer*.
    b. *The Pioneers*.
    c. *The Last of the Mohicans*.
    d. all of the above

13. Washington Irving is the author of

    a. *Tales of a Traveler*.
    b. "Rip Van Winkle."
    c. "The Legend of Sleepy Hollow."
    d. all of the above

14. The landscape paintings of _____ established the image of the American
    West as a romantic and wild place.

    a. Albert Bierstadt
    b. Nathaniel Hawthorne
    c. Matthew Brady
    d. all of the above

15. Which of the following did <u>not</u> occur in education in the 1800s?

    a. The first public high schools were established in New York.
    b. The Western world's first women's college was established in the U.S.
    c. Coeducation spread through U.S. graduate schools.
    d. Thomas Jefferson founded the Library of Congress.

Content Cluster: FOREIGN POLICY IN THE EARLY REPUBLIC

Objectives: To evaluate the student's understanding of: (1) the political and economic causes and consequences of the War of 1812, (2) the Monroe Doctrine and America's relations with Mexico, Canada, and Europe, and (3) major treaties with the Indian nations between 1789 and 1816.

Parent Tip:　This cluster focuses on the difficulties faced by the new nation as it struggled to find its way among the major world powers of the nineteenth century. Encourage your child to make charts and timelines to clarify events and to track the ebb and flow of tensions that existed among the United States, Great Britain, France, and Spain. During this period, the nationalistic spirit that led the U.S. in its dealings with foreign nations permeated its relations with the Native Americans on their own soil. In 1789, one of the first declarations of the U.S. Congress stated:

> The utmost good faith shall always be observed toward the Indians, their lands and property shall never be taken from them without their consent; and their property, rights, and liberty, they shall never be invaded or disturbed, unless in just and lawful wars authorized by congress; but laws founded in justice and humanity shall from time to time be made, for preventing wrongs being done to them, and for preserving peace and friendship with them.

The Westward expansion of the United States in the 1800s was at direct odds with this policy statement. The story of the Native Americans was one of coercion that culminated in the forced exile of an entire people through the Indian Removal Act of 1830. The advantage of hindsight affords us the opportunity to review historic decisions and to ask ourselves whether we would have made the same choices. Encourage your children to ask themselves if they had been the decision makers, might the course of history have been different?

Choose the best answer.

1. In the 1800s, the term *impressment* referred to

    a. an attitude of arrogance among members of the press.
    b. a financial arrangement among the wealthy merchants and landowners.
    c. a practice used by the British to force men into being sailors in the navy.
    d. none of the above

2. Impressment caused problems for the United States because

    a. the press criticized the U.S. Navy without reason.
    b. the banking industry continually argued with the farmers.
    c. American civilians were captured by the British and taken to sea to work on British warships.
    d. none of the above

3. Which of the following is <u>not</u> considered a cause of the War of 1812?

    a. impressment and British attacks on U.S. merchant ships
    b. Britain provided Native Americans with arms on the frontier.
    c. the desire to expand U.S. territory to include Canada and Spanish Florida
    d. a growing sense of isolationism

4. The "war hawks" of the West were led by _____. They were _____ entering into war with Britain in 1812.

    a. Henry Clay and John C. Calhoun / in favor of
    b. Henry Clay and John C. Calhoun / against
    c. Zebulon Pike and Toussaint l'Ouverture / afraid of
    d. Meriwether Lewis and William Clark / outspoken about

5. As a war strategy, the United States planned

    a. a three-pronged attack on Canada: from Lake Champlain to Montreal, across the Niagara frontier, and from Detroit to Upper Canada.
    b. to defeat Napoleon and take his riches for the American war chest.
    c. the collapse of Fort Detroit and Fort Dearborn in the frontier.
    d. all of the above

6. When American troops tried to conquer Canada at the beginning of the War of 1812,

    a. the Canadians ignored the threat because most of the population was French.
    b. they were overcome by British-Canadian troops and 1,000 of Chief Tecumsah's braves.
    c. the U.S. army was large, strong, and well-organized.
    d. the state militias gave their complete support to joining in the fight.

7. During the War of 1812, the U.S. Navy

    a. was joined by a group of privateers that captured British merchant ships.
    b. consisted of 14 ships and was outnumbered by more than 1,000 British ships that formed a blockade.
    c. won some spectacular victories, thanks to the frigate *Constitution*, or "Old Ironsides."
    d. all of the above

8. The British blockade

    a. had little effect on the American economy.
    b. angered the Native Americans who wanted to enter the fur trade.
    c. brought American trade to a virtual halt and the U.S. economy to the verge of collapse.
    d. none of the above

9. Which of the following quotations arose from the War of 1812?

    a. "Don't give up the ship" –Captain James Lawrence aboard the *Chesapeake*
    b. "We have met the enemy and they are ours."—Oliver Hazard Perry of the *Niagra*
    c. "Now, boys, pour it into them."—Captain Isaac Hull aboard the *Constitution*
    d. all of the above

10. In 1814, the situation looked bleak for the United States because

    a. Britain defeated Napoleon and could turn its full attention to the war with the United States.
    b. the war was causing great economic damage to the Northeast.
    c. the British had burned the public buildings of Washington, D.C., including the White House, and were heading for Chesapeake Bay.
    d. all of the above

11. The Battle of Fort McHenry

    a. was the main defense of the Mississippi River.
    b. was the inspiration for "The Star-Spangled Banner."
    c. was held to defend South Carolina.
    d. gave the British a stunning defeat over the United States.

12. The British strategy to win the War of 1812 included

    a. an attack from Canada into the frontier, which was abandoned after the American victory on Lake Champlain.
    b. an attack into the Middle States, which was thwarted by the Battle of Fort McHenry
    c. an assault on New Orleans and the Gulf Coast, which ended with Andrew Jackson's victory two weeks after the war was ended.
    d. all of the above

13. Which of the following was <u>not</u> a consequence of the War of 1812?

    a. The Federalist Party lost its influence.
    b. Andrew Jackson became a national hero after the Battle of New Orleans.
    c. The problems of impressment, neutrality, and the Canadian-American border were resolved immediately.
    d. Native Americans in the upper Midwest were no longer a threat to U.S. westward expansion.

14. After 1815, diplomacy between the United States and Great Britain

    a. fixed the border between the U.S. and Canada.
    b. provided for their joint control of the Oregon Country.
    c. provided that neither country would maintain a fleet of warships on the Great Lakes.
    d. all of the above

15. Which of the following gave rise to the Monroe Doctrine?

    a. Several of Spain's colonies in Latin America won their independence, and Spain wanted to reclaim them.
    b. The War of 1812 awarded Texas and Florida to the United States.
    c. The War of 1812 caused an economic depression.
    d. all of the above

16. Which of the following principles was <u>not</u> set forth in the Monroe Doctrine?

    a. The United States intended to become involved in European affairs and participate in European wars.
    b. No more colonies could be founded in the Americas.
    c. The United States would consider any interference by European powers in the Americas a direct threat to U.S. security.
    d. The United States would not interfere with existing colonies of the European nations, such as Canada and Cuba.

17. Among the types of treaties between the United States and the Native Americans were

    a. peace treaties.
    b. land cession treaties from the Native Americans to the United States.
    c. creation of reservations for the Native Americans.
    d. all of the above

18. In 1795, the Treaty of Greenville

    a. was signed after the Battle of Little Bighorn.
    b. was signed by 92 leading chiefs who agreed to turn over to the United States the entire southern half of what is now Ohio.
    c. led to Custer's last stand.
    d. none of the above

19. In 1809, the Treaty of Fort Wayne

    a. placed the Native Americans in a position of economic advantage.
    b. was the final treaty between the Native Americans and the United States.
    c. had the Delaware Indians and 3 other tribes cede approximately 3 million acres in return for annuities ranging from $200 - $500 to each tribe.
    d. led to Custer's last stand.

Content Cluster: DIVERGENT PATHS OF THE AMERICANS: THE NORTHEASTERNERS

Objectives: To evaluate the student's understanding of: (1) how industrialization and technological developments affected the Northeast, (2) the Irish immigration, (3) the lives of free black Americans in the North, (4) the development of the American education system and the women's suffrage movement, and (5) American art and literature of the first half of the nineteenth century.

Parent Tip: Historians have opined that it was not until after the War of 1812 that the Americans began to achieve a native culture that was distinctly American. Authors, artists, and educators of the first half of the nineteenth century helped to define the common American experience. Share with your child selections from the giants of American literature that dramatized our history—Ralph Waldo Emerson, Henry David Thoreau, Nathaniel Hawthorne, Walt Whitman, Emily Dickinson, Henry Wadsworth Longfellow, and Herman Melville. Try to make history come alive for your children. Help them to imagine the enormous differences in life before and after the Industrial Revolution and the Transportation Revolution.

Choose the best answer.

1. Between 1790 and 1840 the United States underwent profound changes, including

   a. its physical size had doubled in area, and its population had grown from 4 million to 17 million people.
   b. a change from 90% of Americans working as farmers, to 60% engaged in farming by 1840.
   c. The number of people living in towns grew from 5% to 11%
   d. all of the above

2. A diversified economy in the United States in the 1800s refers to

   a. the extension of credit to the rich and the poor.
   b. a combination of farming and manufacturing within the nation.
   c. a desire to be dependent on one crop for export to foreign nations.
   d. none of the above

3. The Industrial Revolution refers to

   a. a rejection of mechanical instruments in favor of natural implements.
   b. a continuous rise in prices that spirals out of control.
   c. a change in production methods from human to machine power.
   d. a secret coup that was planned by the urbanized states.

4. Which of the following was <u>not</u> a factor that contributed to the urbanization pattern of the Northeast?

   a. Machines run by waterpower required factories to be located by lakes, rivers, and waterfalls.
   b. The Northeasterners were dedicated to farming because of the region's fertile soil.
   c. The factory system replaced the domestic system in the early 1800s.
   d. The first mills were established in the New England states.

5. Henry Clay's vision of the American System included

   a. a protective tariff for American manufacturing.
   b. a national system of roads and canals to encourage commerce between farmers and consumers.
   c. authorization of a Second National Bank to finance road, canal, and harbor construction, and to provide credit to developing industries.
   d. all of the above

6. James Monroe opposed federally built roads to link the West to other parts of the nation because

   a. he did not believe the Constitution authorized such action.
   b. he saw no need to increase the sectionalism of the nation.
   c. he thought the projects were too expensive.
   d. all of the above

7. The Cumberland Road

   a. was the first attempt to link the eastern regions of the U.S. to the western regions.
   b. was a private turnpike that charged travelers a heavy toll.
   c. was rarely used after it was built, because it had no bridges over river crossings.
   d. was unpaved and avoided the Appalachian Mountains.

8. The Erie Canal

   a. was an expensive experiment that failed to produce any profit.
   b. failed to connect the Great Lakes to the Atlantic Coast.
   c. passed through the Mohawk Valley and a gap in the Appalachian Mountains in New York.
   d. was the last canal to complete a network of canals throughout the country that served to stimulate farming and manufacturing.

9. The Transportation Revolution of the 1800s

    a. included the development of a web of turnpikes, canals, steamboats, and railroads.
    b. provided a great economic boost to the entire country.
    c. created an expansion of business opportunities throughout the nation.
    d. all of the above

10. In the 1840s, immigrants to the United States

    a. were mostly wealthy investors and protestant ministers who settled in the country.
    b. came from Ireland because of the Great Famine that was caused by a disease that destroyed its potato crops.
    c. were welcomed with open arms by the nativists.
    d. were immediately welcomed because of their affiliation with the Catholic Church.

11. Among the free black Americans who lived in the North were

    a. Benjamin Banneker, a mathematician who also wrote a popular almanac.
    b. William Wells Brown, the first African American novelist and playwright.
    c. abolitionists Henry Highland Garnet, Charles Remond, and Frederick Douglass.
    d. all of the above

12. Educational reformers such as Horace Mann, Thaddeus Stevens, and Henry Barnard

    a. called for free public schools to promote an educated electorate.
    b. supported public schools to prevent social ills like poverty and crime.
    c. were opposed by those who did not want the government to levy taxes to pay for public education.
    d. all of the above

13. Women's suffrage was espoused by

    a. Lucretia Mott, who organized the Women's Rights Convention At Seneca Falls, New York.
    b. abolitionists like Elizabeth Cady Stanton, who the male delegates would not allow to participate in an international antislavery conference in London in 1840.
    c. Susan B. Anthony, who argued for equal pay for women teachers and for equal property rights for women.
    d. all of the above

14. Transcendentalism

    a.   was a philosophy and literary movement that emphasized the unity of human beings and nature, the value of intuition over reason, and the importance of self-reliance and individual conscience.

    b.   was publicized by Ralph Waldo Emerson, Henry David Thoreau, Bronson Alcott, and Margaret Fuller in the *Dial.*

    c.   provided support for reform in America, particularly the antislavery movement.

    d.   all of the above

15. American art of the 1800s

    a.   was very realistic and anti-American in theme.

    b.   portrayed the gritty slums of the cities.

    c.   was typified by the Hudson River School that painted romantic landscapes of the river valley.

    d.   all of the above

Content Cluster: DIVERGENT PATHS OF THE AMERICANS:
THE SOUTHERNERS

Objectives: To evaluate the student's understanding of: (1) the agrarian economy in the South and the significance of cotton; (2) the origins and development of slavery, its effects on black Americans and on all aspects of life in the South, and the strategies that were tried to both overturn and preserve it; (3) white Southern society prior to the Civil War; and (4) the differences between the lives of free blacks in the North and free blacks in the South.

Parent Tip: After the American Revolution, slavery seemed to be dying out. The northern states had passed laws abolishing it, organized religion argued against the institution, and in 1808 Congress prohibited bringing any more slaves into the United States. Great Britain outlawed the slave trade in 1807 and abolished slavery altogether in 1833. The emerging nations of South America prohibited slavery, and Spain and Portugal abolished slave trading in 1840. But after the invention of the cotton gin, cotton production in the southern United States greatly increased the demand for slaves and land. As a result, slavery did not die; it lived to divide the nation. Consider the words of poet William Cullin Bryant after the Supreme Court ruled in the Dred Scott case that Congress had no power to exclude slavery from the territories:

> Hereafter, if this decision shall stand for law, slavery, instead of being
> what the people of the slave states have hitherto called it, their peculiar
> institution, is a Federal institution, the common patrimony and shame
> of all the states, those which flaunt the title of free, as well as those
> which accept the stigma of being the Land of Bondage; hereafter,
> wherever our jurisdiction extends, it carries with it the chain and
> the scourge—wherever our flag floats, it is the flag of slavery.
> If so, that flag should have the light of the stars and the streaks of
> morning red erased from it; it should be dyed black, and its device
> should be the ship and the fetter. Are we to accept, without question,
> these new readings of the Constitution . . . ? Never! Never!

Choose the best answer.

1. Between 1790 and 1840 the United States underwent profound changes, including

   a. its physical size had doubled in area, and its population had grown from 4 million to 17 million people.
   b. a change from 90% of Americans working as farmers, to 60% engaged in farming by 1840.
   c. The number of people living in towns grew from 5% to 11%.
   d. all of the above

2.　The cotton gin

    a.　was a very expensive machine that only a few farmers could afford.

    b.　was a machine that used a toothed cylinder to separate cottonseed from the
       cotton fiber.

    c.　made it possible for one person to remove the seeds from 50 pounds of cotton a
       day, versus 1 pound a day without the cotton gin.

    d.　choices *b* and *c* only

3.　Cotton

    a.　was the only crop grown in the South.

    b.　farming in the South grew from 10,000 bales in 1793 to a production of more
       than 1,000,000 bales in 1835.

    c.　plants needed little care once they had been planted.

    d.　all of the above

4.　Which of the following is <u>not</u> a true statement about the South by 1850?

    a.　Tobacco was the most important crop in Maryland, Virginia, and North
       Carolina, but cotton was the main crop in South Carolina, Georgia, Alabama,
       Tennessee, and Mississippi.

    b.　The majority of wealth and land in the South was concentrated in the hands of
       relatively few plantation owners.

    c.　Three-quarters of the white families had no slaves and worked on their own
       small farms.

    d.　99% of the southern population had plantations with 40 or more slaves.

5.　After the cotton gin arrived on the scene in 1800 and cotton became more profitable,

    a.　the slaves were considered more valuable property, so their living conditions
       improved somewhat.

    b.　less slaves were freed by their owners.

    c.　owners tended to try to make their slaves work harder because the high price of
       cotton encouraged them to increase production by any means.

    d.　all of the above

6.　In support of slavery, Southerners argued that

    a.　"Cotton is King," and the national economy would collapse without slave labor
       to produce cotton.

    b.　it was unpatriotic to criticize slavery.

    c.　slavery was good for slaves because they didn't have to beg like poor urban free
       workers in the North.

    d.　all of the above

7. Abolitionists

    a. argued that slavery was contrary to the American political principle that all men are created equal, as well as the religious belief that all human beings are equal in the eyes of God.
    b. generally repudiated the Transcendentalist philosophy.
    c. were not considered radical in their day.
    d. all of the above

8. Which of the following people did <u>not</u> plot a slave uprising?

    a. Gabriel Prosser of Richmond Virginia
    b. William Lloyd Garrison of the Anti-Slavery Society
    c. Denmark Vesey of Charleston, South Carolina
    d. Nat Turner of Southampton County, Virginia

9. After Nat Turner's revolt,

    a. Southern planters urged their slaves to read the Bible.
    b. in most states it was illegal to teach a slave to read, and anyone caught doing it could be put to death.
    c. there was a sharp increase in the education and literacy of slaves.
    d. slave marriages were recognized in the South, and slave testimony became legal in court.

10. Free blacks in the North

    a. had no opportunity to speak out against slavery.
    b. such as Paul Cuffe, had little economic opportunity.
    c. such as Henry Highland Garnet, could speak openly about the evil of slavery.
    d. unanimously agreed about the specifics of the best solution to the slavery problem.

11. Harriet Tubman

    a. made 19 trips into the South as a conductor on the Underground Railroad and helped nearly 300 slaves escape to freedom.
    b. was called the President of the Underground Railroad.
    c. was born a free woman in Philadelphia and published an abolitionist newspaper.
    d. all of the above

Content Cluster: DIVERGENT PATHS OF THE AMERICANS:
THE WESTERNERS

Objectives: To evaluate the student's understanding of: (1) the election of 1828 and the era of Jacksonian democracy, (2) the westward expansion and Manifest Destiny, (3) the role of women in the West, (4) the struggle over water rights, and (5) the Texas War for Independence and the Mexican American War.

Parent Tip: The move of Americans across the continent from the Atlantic to the Pacific had a profound influence on the American character. With every push west, Americans became more independent, with a spirit that favored self-reliance and self-determination. Little thought was given to manners or culture, for leisure time was scarce. But the community spirit was strong, and this made economic, social, and political arrangements more democratic.

The settling of the frontier occurred in different stages. First, the Eastern Seaboard was settled. (Maine was frontier country for a generation after the Revolutionary War.) The second frontier was the region just west of the Appalachians. Then, by the 1800s, the Mississippi and Ohio valleys became a third great frontier region. By the 1840s, families began traveling by the hundreds across the plains and mountains over the Oregon Trail. The prevailing attitude during the final frontier push was that the United States was destined to dominate the entire continent, from shore to shore.

The picture was not altogether rosy. The Native Americans suffered repeatedly throughout the nation's expansion. Under the administration of Andrew Jackson, the government removed the Indians from their lifelong homelands in the East—by breaking treaties that had previously granted them the right to live on their lands forever—and sent them to present-day Oklahoma. In addition, the westward expansion merely aggravated the slavery question. America's difficulties grew with its size.

Choose the best answer.

1.   Andrew Jackson's election to the Presidency in 1828 was significant because

    a. it continued the tradition of electing candidates who were born in Virginia or New England.
    b. it signaled the death of the Democratic Party.
    c. he brought a greater degree of democracy to American government.
    d. all of the above

2. *Laissez-faire* refers to

   a. a fair and just punishment in a criminal trial.
   b. an economic policy of not interfering with commerce or market forces.
   c. consistent, strong government regulation of commerce.
   d. a kind of barter system where people exchange goods and services in an outdoor market.

3. Jacksonian democracy

   a. saw a rise in the political participation of the common man.
   b. demanded allegiance to the abolitionist movement.
   c. was the strongest supporter of the American System of internal improvements.
   d. all of the above

4. Jackson introduced the "spoils system,"

   a. a plan to abolish slavery in the West through gerrymandering.
   b. a plan to pick up the garbage from the city streets by enacting a federal tax.
   c. a form of political patronage that rewarded Jackson's supporters with government jobs.
   d. a plan to destroy the national bank.

5. President Jackson

   a. renewed the charter of the Second Bank of the United States.
   b. believed that the national bank was a constitutional exercise of governmental powers.
   c. vetoed the bill to recharter the Second Bank of the United States and withdrew all federal money from it.
   d. supported the Second Bank of the United States because he believed it was run by the wealthy and had great influence on economic policy.

6. President Jackson's policy toward the Native Americans

   a. exhibited patience, understanding, and respect for their culture and history.
   b. centered around a policy of their removal from their homelands.
   c. did not affect lands that were previously granted to them by treaty.
   d. none of the above

7. In response to the removal policy, the Cherokees appealed to the U. S. Supreme Court to protest state sanctioned seizure of their property and their prejudicial treatment in state and local courts. Which of the following is <u>not</u> a true statement?

    a. The Supreme Court ruled in favor of Georgia, thus setting the stage for the Trail of Tears.

    b. The Supreme Court ruled in favor of the Cherokees, and the name of the case was *Worcester v. Georgia.*

    c. President Jackson refused to use federal power to enforce the Supreme Court's decision.

    d. Chief Justice John Marshall declared Georgia's persecution of the Native Americans was unconstitutional.

8. *Manifest destiny* refers to

    a. the concept that the United States must convert the Native Americans to Christianity.

    b. the justification for the United States expansion into the Southwest and Far West.

    c. the resurgence of religious fervor in the United States.

    d. the movement for free public education for all people in the United States.

9. After Mexico achieved its independence from Spain in 1821,

    a. there were few Mexicans living in Texas, so the Mexican government encouraged Americans to settle East Texas.

    b. the Mexican government supported the importation of slaves into Texas.

    c. the Mexican government successfully suppressed Texas's revolt for independence.

    d. the Lone Star Republic led an aggressive campaign to conquer the Mexico.

10. The United States annexed Texas in 1845

    a. and never had any problems with Mexico over the border.

    b. as a result of the Bear Flag Revolt in Texas.

    c. over the objections of the Whigs, who opposed slavery.

    d. and led to the battle of the Alamo.

11. In the Treaty of Guadalupe Hildalgo that ended the war with Mexico,

    a. the United States paid $15 million for territory known as the Mexican Cession.

    b. the United States received Mexican territory that included the future states of California, Nevada, Utah, most of New Mexico and Arizona, and parts of Wyoming and Colorado.

    c. set the U.S.-Mexican border at the Rio Grande River.

    d. all of the above

12. Pioneer women

    a. were not essential to the development of the West, because they had no political power.

    b. were allowed to own property and vote once they reached their western destinations.

    c. were not allowed to do any work typically done by men.

    d. typically prepared meals, washed clothes, cared for their children, drove oxen teams, gathered buffalo chips for fuel, and shared additional chores with men on a daily basis.

13. Which of the following is <u>not</u> a true statement about Annie Bidwell?

    a. She was a civic leader, philanthropist, suffragist, and temperance reformer in California.

    b. She never married out of a matter of principle, believing that women should not yield any power to men, and became a senator in California.

    c. She explored California and founded Chico with her husband, U.S. Senator John Bidwell.

    d. She worked to improve education and funded causes such as women's rights, Indian rights, and election reform.

14. Brigham Young and the Mormons who settled in Salt Lake City

    a. changed the concept of the law applicable to water rights, in order to support community, agriculture, and irrigation.

    b. utilized the existing Law of Riparian Rights to build dams and irrigation systems.

    c. argued against the Law of Prior Appropriation on the basis that individual need outweighed the good of the community

    d. all of the above

15. The discovery of gold at Sutter's Mill in January 1848

    a. made all of the 49ers who came to California very rich.

    b. elevated the status of Mexican Californians, Native Americans, free blacks, and Chinese Americans, because everyone in the region was a prospector.

    c. brought so many settlers to California that it became a state in 1850.

    d. all of the above

16. The land grant system of Mexico

    a.   established huge ranchos that were given to business people who attracted more settlers.
    b.   was used extensively to colonize Texas and California with Americans.
    c.   was supported by a system of ranchos, presidios, and missions.
    d.   all of the above

17. With respect to class systems and slavery, which statement accurately describes the Mexican settlements?

    a.   There were no class distinctions recognized in the Mexican culture.
    b.   The Spanish, Creoles, Mestizos, and Indians shared equal economic and political power.
    c.   Although slavery was strictly outlawed in the republic of Mexico, American settlers found ways to keep their slaves in Texas.
    d.   Americans who moved to the Mexican province of Texas engaged in manufacturing and had little need for slaves.

18. The Lone Star Republic

    a.   was established as a result of the Bear Flag Revolt.
    b.   was settled as a result of the Gold Rush in 1849.
    c.   was annexed by the United States after the election of James K. Polk.
    d.   all of the above

Content Cluster: THE ABOLITIONIST MOVEMENT

Objectives: To evaluate the student's understanding of: (1) attempts to abolish slavery in the United States, and (2) the abolitionist movement.

> **Parent Tip:** In the 1800s, the abolitionists who argued that slavery ought to be abolished, were considered dangerous radicals. This seemed so because even the greatest minds of the country could not envision a legal way to end slavery without another revolution or civil war. Under the Constitution, each state decided whether to allow slavery within its borders. Although the northern states did not permit it, slavery supported the southern states to the point that their citizens would never voluntarily agree to free their slaves. What about a Constitutional amendment to abolish slavery? By 1850, half of the 30 states in the nation permitted slavery. But an amendment to the Constitution would need to be ratified by two-thirds of the states. Thus, to urge America to abolish slavery under these circumstances was tantamount to urging a revolt or civil war.

Choose the best answer.

1. The _____ were among the earliest foes of slavery.

    a. indentured servants
    b. owners of small farms
    c. Quakers
    d. plantation owners

2. The Northwest Ordinance of 1787

    a. declared that the land north of the Ohio River and east of the Mississippi should be without slaves.
    b. was the first national stand against slavery.
    c. established that a part of the proceeds from the government's sale of land to individuals would support local schools.
    d. all of the above

3. The Missouri Compromise of 1820

    a. allowed Missouri to enter the Union as a slave state and Maine to enter as a free state.
    b. was reached when Missouri petitioned Congress for admission to the Union as a slaveholding state at a time when there was an equal balance of slave states and free states.
    c. provided that with the exception of Missouri, no slavery would be allowed in the Louisiana Territory north of latitude 36° 30'.
    d. all of the above

4. John Quincy Adams

    a. became an advocate against slavery as a congressman after his term as President.
    b. founded *The Liberator* in Boston.
    c. published *The Genius of Universal Emancipation.*
    d. none of the above

5. Theodore Weld

    a. was among the most radical abolitionists who favored immediate emancipation of all slaves and urged northern states to secede from the United States.
    b. was among the more moderate abolitionists who favored "immediate abolition gradually achieved."
    c. was married to Angelina Grimké, who urged southern women to take a stand against slavery.
    d. choices *b* and *c* only

6. William Lloyd Garrison

    a. was among the more moderate abolitionists who favored "immediate abolition gradually achieved."
    b. was among the most radical abolitionists who favored immediate emancipation of all slaves and urged northern states to secede from the United States.
    c. published *The Liberator* and founded the American Anti-Slavery Society.
    d. choices *b* and *c* only

7. Frederick Douglass

    a. was a slave that escaped to freedom and settled in Massachusetts.
    b. was a persuasive African American abolitionist agent of the American Anti-Slavery Society.
    c. published the abolitionist newspaper, *The North Star.*
    d. all of the above

8. Harriet Tubman

    a. made 19 trips into the South as a conductor on the Underground Railroad and helped nearly 300 slaves escape to freedom.
    b. wrote *Uncle Tom's Cabin* based on her meeting with Simon Legrree.
    c. was born a free woman in Philadelphia and published an abolitionist newspaper.
    d. all of the above

9. The Underground Railroad

    a. was a tunnel of buried train cars that ran along state borders.

    b. was an informal organization that helped slaves hide in safe houses as they escaped to Canada.

    c. was a secret organization that supported slavery in the northern states.

    d. was an organization committed to the arrest and conviction of abolitionists.

10. John Brown

    a. died in shame, hated by the abolitionists and most northerners.

    b. intended to seize land in a remote area of the North to start a commune.

    c. led an attack on the U.S. government armory in Harper's Ferry, Virginia.

    d. choices *b* and *c* only

11. The Wilmot Proviso of 1846

    a. called for the prohibition of slavery in any territory taken from Mexico.

    b. easily passed the House of Representatives due to its subject matter.

    c. was introduced and supported by the Southerners.

    d. none of the above

12. California's petition for admission to the Union led to the _____ in which it was admitted as a _____ state.

    a. destruction of slavery / free

    b. establishment of the Bear Flag Republic / slave

    c. Compromise of 1850 / free

    d. Compromise of 1850 / slave

13. In the Compromise of 1850

    a. the people of New Mexico and Utah would decide by popular sovereignty (vote) whether they wanted to be slave or free.

    b. to appease the South, Congress passed a strong Fugitive Slave Law that strictly forbade Northerners to grant refuge to escaped slaves.

    c. the slave trade was abolished in Washington, D.C.

    d. all of the above

14. Henry Clay, the Great Compromiser, worked out which of the following compromises to ease sectional conflicts?

    a.   the American System, in which western Congressmen voted for high tariffs in exchange for eastern votes for internal improvements to help move western goods to market.

    b.   the Missouri Compromise, in which Missouri was admitted as a slave state, and Maine was separated from Massachusetts and admitted as a free state.

    c.   the Compromise of 1850, a series of five bills that dealt with the slavery issue in the Southwest and Far West.

    d.   all of the above

15. The Kansas-Nebraska Act of 1854

    a.   arose as a result of the territories of Kansas and Nebraska applying for statehood.

    b.   left the question of slavery in Kansas and Nebraska up to popular sovereignty, thus flooding the territory with people on both sides of the slavery issue that wanted to influence the election result.

    c.   repealed the Missouri Compromise prohibition on slavery imposed on that region.

    d.   all of the above

16. In *Dred Scott v. Sandford*, the majority opinion of the U.S. Supreme Court

    a.   considered the case of a slave who sued for his freedom in a Missouri court after his master took him to Illinois and the free territory of Wisconsin.

    b.   ruled against Scott, stating that a black man had no rights as a citizen and that he was merely his owner's property.

    c.   argued that under the Fifth Amendment, Congress had no right to deprive citizens of their property (slaves) anywhere within the United States.

    d.   all of the above

17. The Lincoln-Douglas debates

    a.   centered around the slavery question, with Douglas trying to paint Lincoln as a radical abolitionist, and Lincoln trying to portray Douglas as a pro-slavery supporter of the Dred Scott case.

    b.   were held to decide who would be elected President.

    c.   had Lincoln arguing for the states' right to decide the slavery issue.

    d.   Resulted in Lincoln winning the Illinois Senate race.

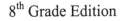

Content Cluster: THE CIVIL WAR

Objectives: To evaluate the student's understanding of the multiple causes, key events, and complex consequences of the Civil War.

> **Parent Tip:** Historians debate the reasons why the South seceded at the moment it did. Even with the election of the "black Republican," Abraham Lincoln, as President, there was little chance that the South or slavery stood in real danger. Had the South remained in the Union, Lincoln would have faced a hostile majority in Congress. Moreover, southerners dominated the Supreme Court. Given the requirement of an approval by two-thirds of the states, a Constitutional Amendment prohibiting slavery was out of the question. In any event, Lincoln and other moderates had no intention of trying to destroy slavery where it already existed. Lincoln's hands were tied to accomplish any change on the slavery issue. This has led many historians to conclude that southerners simply could not accept the idea that their system was "wrong," and that their regional loyalty was much stronger than their loyalty to the entire United States.
>
> This period in history provides several topics for discussion that have relevance to politics today, including states' rights, economic dominance, the political aspects of Supreme Court decisions, segregation, and racial prejudice.

Choose the best answer.

1. John C. Calhoun

    a. argued on several occasions that a state was obligated to obey the federal law, regardless of its constitutionality.
    b. argued on several occasions that a state had a right to refuse to obey any federal law that it believed to be unconstitutional.
    c. never held national elective office because of his federalist views.
    d. was an opponent of the nullification doctrine.

2. The doctrine of nullification

    a. arose in connection with tariffs during Andrew Jackson's administration.
    b. was set forth by Thomas Jefferson in opposition to the Alien and Sedition Acts.
    c. is premised upon the importance of states' rights.
    d. all of the above

3. Regarding the issue of slavery in 1850,

    a. John C. Calhoun argued that citizens had the right to take their property (slaves) into all territories of the United States, including new lands acquired from Mexico.

    b. Daniel Webster argued for peace and unity of the nation, not as a northerner, but as an American, in support of a compromise.

    c. Henry Clay looked beyond sectional demands to forge a compromise that made both sides give up something they wanted.

    d. all of the above

4. "Mr. President, I wish to speak to-day, not as a Massachusetts man, nor as a northern man, but as an American, and as a member of the Senate of the United States. . . . I speak to-day for the preservation of the Union. . . . There has been found in the North, among individuals and among legislators, a disinclination to perform fully their constitutional duties in regard to the return of persons bound to service [fugitive slaves] who have escaped into the free States. In that respect, the South, in my judgment, is right, and the North is wrong." These are the words of

    a. Thomas Jefferson
    b. John C. Calhoun
    c. Daniel Webster
    d. Abraham Lincoln

5. "How can the Union be saved? There is but one way by which it can with any certainty; and that is, by a full and final settlement, on the principle of justice, of all the questions at issue between the [North and South]. The South asks for justice, simple justice, and less she ought not to take. She has no compromise to offer but the Constitution; and no concession or surrender to make. She has already surrendered so much she has little left to surrender. . . .The North has only to will it to accomplish it—to do justice by conceding to the South an equal right in the acquired territory, and to do her duty by causing stipulations [rules] relative to fugitive slaves to be faithfully fulfilled. . . .At all events, the responsibility for saving the Union rests on the North, and not on the South." These are the words of

    a. Thomas Jefferson
    b. John C. Calhoun
    c. Daniel Webster
    d. Abraham Lincoln

6. "If slavery is not wrong, nothing is wrong." These are the words of

    a. Thomas Jefferson
    b. John C. Calhoun
    c. Daniel Webster
    d. Abraham Lincoln

7. By 1860, the North and South had grown into sections that were widely unlike

   a. because the South was almost totally rural, with only New Orleans as a city of considerable size, and the North was thriving on shipbuilding, iron, and textile industries in the midst of several urban centers.
   b. because the South had an enormous number of immigrants that settled there to compete against slave labor.
   c. because the South contained the best transportation and the most railroad links to other areas of the country.
   d. because an increasing number of southerners supported protective tariffs, while northerners, wanting cheap imported manufactured goods, strongly opposed them.

8. Geographically, the North and South differed in that

   a. seaports were essential to the South from the beginning, because ships could not sail up their shallow rivers and waterfalls.
   b. the people of the South were more isolated because large, self-sufficient estates spread along the broad, deep rivers upon which ocean vessels could sail.
   c. The southerners were very community minded and gathered in towns where they had town meetings and educated their children in public schools.
   d. all of the above

9. Which of the following Constitutional issues was posed by succession of the South?

   a. Since the states existed separately before they joined to form the United States and they drafted the Constitution, did they have the right to withdraw whenever they pleased?
   b. as the supreme law of the land, did the Constitution overrule states' rights?
   c. both of the above
   d. none of the above

10. The Confederate States of America consisted of

   a. South Carolina, Georgia, Louisiana, Mississippi, Florida, Alabama, Texas, Virginia, Tennessee, Arkansas, and North Carolina.
   b. South Carolina, Georgia, Louisiana, Mississippi, Florida, Alabama, and Texas.
   c. Maryland, Virginia, North Carolina, South Carolina, Georgia, and Florida
   d. California, Texas, Missouri, Virginia, North Carolina, South Carolina, and Georgia.

11. Jefferson Davis

    a. was elected to be president of a confederacy of independent states, not a union.
    b. had previously served as Vice President of the United States.
    c. never served in the military or held public office before the Civil War.
    d. was charismatic, charming, and an inspirational speaker.

Exercises 12 – 21 contain excerpts of the famous addresses or writings of Abraham Lincoln. In each exercise, identify the quoted passage. Select the best answer from the following choices:

    a. Address to Illinois Delegates (1858)
    b. First Inaugural Address (1861)
    c. Gettysburg Address (1863)
    d. Emancipation Proclamation (1863)
    e. Second Inaugural Address (1865)

12. "Four score and seven year ago our fathers brought forth on this continent a new nation, conceived in liberty, and dedicated to the proposition that all men are created equal. Now we are engaged in a great civil war, testing whether that nation, or any nation so conceived and so dedicated, can long endure. We are met on a great battlefield of that war. We have come to dedicate a portion of that field as a final resting place for those who here gave their lives that that nation might live."

13. "A house divided against itself cannot stand. I believe this government cannot endure permanently half slave and half free. I do not expect the Union to be dissolved – I do not expect the house to fall – but I do expect it will cease to be divided. It will become all one thing, or all the other. Either the opponents of slavery will arrest the further spread of it, and place it where the public mind shall rest in the belief that it is in the course of ultimate extinction; or its advocates will push it forward, till it shall become alike lawful in all the States, old as well as new – North as well as South."

14. "Apprehension seems to exist among the people of the Southern States, that by the accession of a Republican Administration, their property, and their peace, and personal security, are to be endangered. There has never been any reasonable cause for such apprehension. Indeed, the most ample evidence to the contrary has all the while existed, and been open to their inspection. It is found in nearly all the published speeches of him who now addresses you. I do but quote from one of those speeches when I declare that 'I have no purpose, directly or indirectly, to interfere with the institution of slavery in the States where it exists. I believe I have no lawful right to do so, and I have no inclination to do so.'"

15. "Plainly, the central idea of secession, is the essence of anarchy. A majority, held in restraint by constitutional checks, and limitations, and always changing easily with deliberate changes of popular opinions and sentiments, is the only true sovereign of a free people. Whoever rejects it does of necessity, fly to anarchy or to despotism. Unanimity is impossible; the rule of a minority as a permanent arrangement, is wholly inadmissible; so that rejecting the majority principle, anarchy, or despotism in some form is all that is left."

16. "In your hands, my dissatisfied fellow countrymen, and not in mine, is the momentous issue of civil war. The government will not assail you. You can have no conflict, without being yourselves the aggressors. You have no oath registered in Heaven to destroy the government, while I shall have the most solemn one to 'preserve, protect and defend' it. I am loath to close. We are not enemies, but friends. We must not be enemies. Though passion may have strained, it must not break our bonds of affection. The mystic chords of memory, stretching from every battle-field, and patriot grave, to every living hearth and hearthstone, all over this broad land, will yet swell the chorus of the Union, when again touched, as surely they will be, by the better angels of our nature."

17. "The world will little note, nor long remember what we say here, but it can never forget what they did here. It is for us the living, rather, to be dedicated here to the unfinished work which they who fought here have thus far so nobly advanced. It is rather for us to be here dedicated to the great task remaining before us – that from these honored dead we may take increased devotion to that cause for which they gave the last full measure of devotion – that we here highly resolve that these dead shall not have died in vain – that this nation, under God, shall have a new birth of freedom – and that government of the people, by the people, for the people, shall not perish from the earth."

18. "On the occasion corresponding to this four years ago all thoughts were anxiously directed to an impending civil war. All dreaded it; all sought to avert it. While the inaugural address was being delivered from this place, devoted altogether to saving the Union without war, insurgent agents were in the city seeking to destroy it without war – seeking to dissolve the Union and divide effects by negotiation. Both parties deprecated war, but one of them would make war rather than let the nation survive, and the other would accept war rather than let it perish, and the war came. . . .

19. With malice toward none, with charity for all, with firmness in the right as God gives us to see the right, let us strive on to finish the work we are in, to bind up the nation's wounds, to care for him who shall have borne the battle and for his widow and his orphan, to do all which may achieve and cherish a just and lasting peace among ourselves and with all nations. "That on the first day of January, in the year of our Lord one thousand eight hundred and sixty-three, all persons held as slaves within any State, . . . the people whereof shall then be in rebellion against the United States, shall be then, thenceforward, and forever free; and the Executive Government of the United States, including the military and naval authority thereof, will recognize and maintain the freedom of such persons, and will do no act or acts to repress such persons, or any of them, in any efforts they may make for their actual freedom."

Choose the best answer.

20. Robert E. Lee

    a. was Abraham Lincoln's first choice to command the Union Army.
    b. proved more loyal to Virginia than to the nation.
    c. was promptly joined by Southerners who resigned from the U.S. Army
    d. all of the above

21. Ulysses S. Grant

    a. had done poorly in his studies at West Point.
    b. was a shy, slight, extremely brave man, who constantly chewed on a cigar.
    c. proved to be an excellent military strategist.
    d. all of the above

22. In 1860, it appeared that each side would have certain advantages in fighting the war. Which of the following statements is <u>not</u> an accurate description of the factors that could have influenced the war?

    a. The North was far stronger in population, industrial resources, and wealth.
    b. The South had the ability to manufacture all its own war supplies so that it was not dependent upon foreign imports of guns, ammunition, or surgical equipment.
    c. Because the South controlled the world's main cotton supply and Britain needed cotton to keep its mills busy, the South expected Britain to intervene to help it in the war.
    d. Because the South was able to fight a defensive war, its armies had the advantage of operating on inside lines, and it needed only to fight long enough to convince the North that it could not conquer the South.

23. The Emancipation Proclamation

    a. only freed slaves in areas ruled by the Confederates.
    b. only freed slaves who made their way to the free states.
    c. applied to areas in the Confederacy that had been captured by Union armies.
    d. freed all slaves in the Union and the Confederacy.

24. During the war

    a. African American soldiers were not allowed to fight.
    b. 186,000 African American soldiers fought for the United States in 166 all-black regiments.
    c. Abraham Lincoln discouraged African Americans from enlisting in the army.
    d. there was increased racial harmony after the Emancipation Proclamation.

25. Which of the following was <u>not</u> one of President Lincoln's first acts during the war?

    a. to call for 75,000 volunteers to serve in the military for 3 months
    b. to order a naval blockade of southern ports to prevent the exportation of cotton and the importation of munitions and supplies.
    c. to appoint General Stonewall Jackson as the head of the Union Army.
    d. to replace General Winfield Scott with General George B. McClellan.

26. Which of the following is <u>not</u> a true statement about the Battle of Shiloh in Tennessee?

    a. Although Union forces were nearly defeated, reinforcements arrived and drove off the Confederate army.
    b. In 2 days of fighting, 13,000 Union troops and 11,000 Confederate soldiers died.
    c. The combined loss of life at Shiloh was more than the total American casualties in the Revolution, the War of 1812, and the Mexican War, put together.
    d. It was a decisive victory for Stonewall Jackson, after tying up the Union troops for two months.

27. The Second Battle of Bull Run in 1862

    a. marked a low point in the war for the North, because the Union troops had been pushed back from Richmond to Washington.
    b. marked a low point in the war for the South, because the North won its peninsular campaign and captured Richmond.
    c. demonstrated to Lincoln how aggressive his generals could be.
    d. demonstrated that the army with the most soldiers won every battle.

28. Which of the following statements about the Battle of Antietam is <u>not</u> true?

    a. It was won by the South in the deep forest of Tennessee with little loss of life.
    b. It reduced the likelihood that Europe would recognize the South, because it stalled General Lee's march in the North.
    c. It was won by the North after General McClellan intercepted a copy of General Lee's orders detailing troop placement.
    d. It enabled President Lincoln to publish the Emancipation Proclamation from a position of strength.

29. General Ulysses S. Grant and General William Tecumseh Sherman

    a. joined forces to overcome the confederate citadel in Vicksburg, Mississippi.
    b. successfully gained control of the Mississippi River.
    c. effectively split the Confederacy into two parts that could not communicate with each other or send reinforcement .
    d. all of the above

30. Which of the following statements about the Battle of Gettysburg is <u>not</u> true?

    a. It was General Lee's attempt to take the war into Pennsylvania, where a victory would give him a clear road to the Union capital in Washington.
    b. The Confederate army had the advantage of position on high ground, and as a result, suffered few losses.
    c. It was the site of Picket's charge, one of the most gallant efforts in American military history
    d. It had serious consequences for the future because the Confederacy lost one-third of its army's effective strength in the battle.

31. President Lincoln appointed General Grant the head of all the Union armies

    a. because of his great victories at the ports of New Orleans and Mobile.
    b. because of his knowledge of guerrilla warfare.
    c. because unlike other generals who had failed to capitalize on victory, Grant demonstrated tenacity and a willingness to fight and fight again.
    d. because of his brilliant scholastic record at West Point.

32. As commander of all the Union armies, General Grant

    a. began a strategy of attrition, believing that by applying constant pressure on the Confederate forces, his larger armies would eventually overcome Lee's outnumbered men.
    b. was popular with his soldiers because his strategy did not involve much loss of life.
    c. avoided doing battle in the South, preferring instead to fight on Union ground.
    d. uttered the famous words, "Damn the Torpedoes. Full speed ahead!"

33. General Grant put General William Tecumseh Sherman in charge of

    a. a half-hearted attack on a series of Virginia supply routes.
    b. fighting formal battles in the fields, thereby preserving the dignity of the Southern estates and cities.
    c. opposing General Lee's "total war" strategy of destroying the resources of the civilian population as well as fighting formal battles with the armies.
    d. a strategy to split the South horizontally by destroying everything in the path of a march through Georgia to the sea.

34. Which of the following statements does <u>not</u> accurately describe the events that occurred at Appomattox Court House on April 9,1865?

    a. General Lee was dignified in defeat and General Grant was gracious in victory.
    b. General Lee surrendered to General Grant amid such hard feelings that they refused to speak directly to each other.
    c. At President Lincoln's request, General Grant offered generous terms of surrender that allowed Confederates to return home with their horses and sidearms.
    d. General Lee and General Grant shook hands and reminisced about the days when they were colleagues in the army.

35. Which of the following statements does <u>not</u> accurately describe circumstances after the Civil War?

    a. The South was physically, economically, and spiritually devastated.
    b. The war left hatred between North and South that lasted for decades.
    c. The citizens of the North and the South quickly buried the hatchet in an effort to leave the war behind them.
    d. The southern aristocracy was stripped of its wealth and power.

Content Cluster: RECONSTRUCTION

Objectives: To evaluate the student's understanding of: (1) the character and consequences of Reconstruction, and (2) the Thirteenth, Fourteenth, and Fifteenth Amendments to the Constitution.

Parent Tip: Once the South had been defeated, it had to be "reconstructed." Unfortunately, Abraham Lincoln's assassination prevented him from leading the country through the process in the way that he had envisioned it, "with malice toward none, with charity for all." His successor, Andrew Johnson, was a southerner who supported the Fugitive Slave Law and defended slavery. However, when his state of Tennessee seceded from the United States, Johnson rejected the Confederacy and was the only southern senator to remain in the U.S. Senate after secession. Preservation of the Union was of paramount importance to him. As President, however, he was ill equipped to mend the broken nation and help its people cope with emancipation. He was caught between northerners who favored a policy of harsh retribution for the rebellious states, and southerners resistant to giving justice and civil rights to black Americans. Sadly, President Johnson did little to erase the sectional and racial bitterness of the 1800s. What remnants of that heritage still exist today?

Choose the best answer.

1. Which of the following was <u>not</u> a primary purpose of Reconstruction?

    a. to wind up the affairs of the Confederacy and bring the southern states back into the Union
    b. to ensure black Americans their freedom, and civil and political rights
    c. to preserve the health of the U.S. economy
    d. to ease immigration laws to build the population after wartime losses

2. Which of the following was <u>not</u> included in Abraham Lincoln's Reconstruction plan?

    a. provisions to readmit southern states to the Union when their men took loyalty oaths
    b. provisions requiring each southern state to form a government and draft a new constitution that banned slavery,
    c. provisions to give the right to vote to African Americans who had fought for the Union or who had some education
    d. provisions for the states to provide free public education to blacks.

3. The Freedmen's Bureau

   a. helped southern blacks who were homeless and jobless because of the war.
   b. only helped soldiers of the Confederacy.
   c. was established to protect conductors of the Underground Railroad.
   d. was established to help northern widows and orphans.

4. Immediately after the Civil War, most ex-slaves

   a. became sharecroppers on land owned by whites
   b. received some education with assistance from the Freedmen's Bureau
   c. stayed poor, but enjoyed greater freedom over their personal lives.
   d. all of the above

5. In 1866, Congress authorized the creation of 6 regiments of Black troops. The two cavalry regiments became known as the _____ and helped _____.

   a. Scalawags / the Southern post-war economy to recover
   b. Buffalo Soldiers / build forts and roads, and fought the Plains Indians in the West
   c. Infantrymen / guide settlers through the western frontier
   d. Rough Riders / build railroad track and string telegraph lines in the South

6. Southern states that were readmitted to the Union after the Civil War tried to

   a. keep the freedmen subservient by enacting the Black Codes that barred blacks from doing any work except farming and household service.
   b. give the freedmen economic power and political authority in the new society.
   c. please the northern states by electing leaders who had nothing to do with the pre-war aristocracy.
   d. reject the leaders of the Confederacy by banning them from becoming members of either house of Congress.

7. The Thirteenth Amendment to the Constitution

   a. applied the Bill of Rights to actions of the states.
   b. applied the Bill of Rights to actions of the federal government.
   c. abolished slavery everywhere in the United States.
   d. extended the right to vote to black males.

8. The Fourteenth Amendment to the Constitution

   a. applied the Bill of Rights to actions of the states.
   b. applied the Bill of Rights to actions of the federal government.
   c. abolished slavery everywhere in the United States.
   d. extended the right to vote to black males.

9. The Fifteenth Amendment to the Constitution

    a. applied the Bill of Rights to actions of the states.
    b. applied the Bill of Rights to actions of the federal government.
    c. abolished slavery everywhere in the United States.
    d. extended the right to vote to black males.

10. When the southern states refused to ratify the Fourteenth Amendment,

    a. Congress passed the Reconstruction Act, which established military rule in the southern states until they guaranteed black Americans the right to vote and passed the Fourteenth Amendment.
    b. Congress passed a law that forbade sharecroppers from obtaining credit from the national bank.
    c. Congress passed a law that forbade the crop-lien system in the northern states.
    d. all of the above

11. Which of the following was not a means employed in the South to deprive blacks of the right to vote?

    a. poll tax
    b. Freedmen's Bureau
    c. literacy test
    d. grandfather clause

12. The _____ laws of the South extended segregation, or separation of the races, in all public places. They were challenged in the Civil Rights Cases of 1883, and found to be _____ by a majority of the Supreme Court.

    a. Ku Klux Klan / constitutional
    b. Ku Klux Klan / unconstitutional
    c. Jim Crow / constitutional
    d. Jim Crow / unconstitutional

13. The Ku Klux Klan

    a. was determined to keep blacks from voting and influencing politics.
    b. claimed to be the ghosts of Confederate soldiers and terrorized blacks in the night.
    c. were responsible for beating and murdering hundreds of blacks.
    d. all of the above

Content Cluster: The Industrial Revolution

Objectives: To evaluate the student's understanding of: (1) the Industrial Revolution, and (2) its effects on economic, social, and political conditions in the United States.

Parent Tip: After the Civil War, the United States changed dramatically. In 1860, approximately 80% of Americans lived on farms. Of the 31 million people in the nation at that time, less than 1.5 million of them worked in factories. By 1900, however, the population had grown to 76 million, 40% of whom lived in towns and cities. About 5 million people worked in factories at the turn of the century.

Choose the best answer.

1. After the Civil War, Cornelius Vanderbilt

    a. extended the local railroad tracks to connect with each other and facilitated long distance travel and commerce.
    b. opposed the work of the railroad barons who financed the laying of new track.
    c. purchased flour mills and citrus farms all over the nation.
    d. died a poor man because he maintained investments in river shipping to the exclusion of railroad investments.

2. The _____ quickly changed iron to steel and made the mass production of steel a reality. _____ , an American immigrant of humble beginnings, built the largest Bessemer plant in America and became the second richest man in the world.

    a. oil refinery / Samuel M. Kier
    b. Drake's Folly / E.L. Drake
    c. Bessemer converter / Andrew Carnegie
    d. Mesabi Range / Eli Whitney

3. The expense of building railroads led to

    a. the new business arrangement of the corporation.
    b. the abandonment of the industry for many years.
    c. the rise of partnerships to encourage personal liability.
    d. railroad strikes during the Civil War.

4. The growth of the oil industry in the 1850s was based upon a need for

    a. gasoline, diesel fuel, and heating oil.
    b. more whale oil to light lamps.
    c. kerosene to light lamps.
    d. mass production and interchangeable parts.

5. In the 1870s, Alexander Graham Bell invented the _____ , and
   _____ , the Wizard of Menlo Park, invented the phonograph and the
   _____ .

   a. telegraph / Mathew Brady / camera
   b. quadruplex telegraph / Henry Higgins / underground cable
   c. arc light / E.L. Drake / kerosene lamp
   d. telephone / Thomas Edison / incandescent light bulb

In exercises 6 - 10, determine the geographical locations that are connected to one of the natural resources listed below. Select the best answer from the following choices:

   a. coal
   b. oil
   c. iron
   d. copper
   e. silver

6. western Pennsylvania, Texas, Oklahoma, Kansas, Illinois, California

7. Pennsylvania mountains, West Virginia, Illinois, Kansas, Colorado, Texas, New Mexico

8. rim of Lake Superior, Minnesota's Mesabi Range, North Michigan, Tennessee, Colorado

9. Colorado, Nevada, Montana

10. Michigan, Montana, Arizona

Choose the best answer.

11. Which of the following statements does <u>not</u> accurately describe the role of government during the rise of industrialism in the United States?

   a. Congress aggressively regulated private enterprise and industry to maintain fair business practices.
   b. Business interests controlled the national and state legislatures.
   c. The government imposed protective tariffs to eliminate foreign competition.
   d. American companies benefited from government land grants and subsidies.

12. The development of _____, the combining or consolidating businesses to control an industry, made John D. Rockefeller rich in the _____ industry and Commodore Vanderbilt rich in the _____ industry, both of whom were financed by a money trust headed by _____.

    a. corporations / whiskey / money/ Commodore Sloate
    b. trusts / oil refining / railroad / J. P. Morgan
    c. adversarial prosperity / peanut / reaper / national bank
    d. interstate commerce / banking / oil drilling / railroads

13. Immigrants between 1865 and 1880

    a. filled the farms but failed to supply industry with cheap labor.
    b. could not supply laborers to U. S. industry because of a tight immigration policy.
    c. from western and northern Europe contributed to the growth of America's large cities.
    d. from southern and eastern Europe contributed to the growth of America's large cities.

14. After 1880, immigrants

    a. dispersed throughout the country in an effort to become Americanized.
    b. were encouraged to stay and work by the American Protective Association.
    c. joined the Nativist movement to promote their individuality.
    d. from southern and eastern Europe settled in ethnic neighborhoods in the cities.

15. The Knights of Labor

    a. excluded women and blacks from its membership if they were unskilled.
    b. was founded as an industrial union to organize all skilled and unskilled workers in an industry.
    c. excluded immigrants from its membership.
    d. all of the above

16. The American Federation of Labor

    a. excluded women, immigrants, and blacks from its membership if they were unskilled.
    b. was opposed by Samuel Gompers for 37 years.
    c. was founded as an industrial union to organize all unskilled workers in various craft unions.
    d. all of the above

17. Of the 37,000 labor strikes that occurred in the United States between 1881 and 1905,

    a.   three that were especially damaging to organized labor were The Haymarket Riots, the Homestead Strike, and the Pullman Strike.
    b.   many were halted by the company owners through the use of court injunctions.
    c.   many helped workers win the 8-hour workday in several industries.
    d.   all of the above

18. The Grange

    a.   was the first national farmer organization.
    b.   was also known as the Patrons of Husbandry.
    c.   was open to men and women.
    d.   all of the above

19. The Populist Party

    a.   opposed the graduated income tax.
    b.   cared little about farmers or issues relevant to transportation.
    c.   supported farmers and called for government ownership of railroads.
    d.   none of the above

20. After the Civil War, the Bureau of Indian Affairs adopted a policy known as _____ to keep the Native Americans confined to certain areas of the West away from traveling settlers.

    a.   nomadism
    b.   concentration
    c.   Kansas-Nebraska Act
    d.   right of way

21. The search for gold, silver, and copper, and the building of the railroads

    a.   led to the protection of the buffalo on the Indian reservations.
    b.   led to a renewed understanding of the ways of the Plains Indians.
    c.   led to the demise of the buffalo, and with it, the main source of food, clothing, and shelter for the Plains Indians.
    d.   postponed the inevitable wars between the Plains Indians and the U.S. government.

SOCIAL SCIENCE
ANSWER KEY

**Events Preceding
The Founding of
The Nation**
1. d
2. d
3. c
4. b
5. a
6. a
7. d
8. c
9. b
10. b
11. d
12. a

**Political Principles
Underlying the
U.S. Constitution**
1. c
2. a
3. d
4. d
5. a
6. b
7. b
8. a
9. a
10. b
11. d
12. d
13. b
14. b
15. c
16. a
17. a
18. a
19. b
20. a
21. c
22. b
23. c
24. b

25. c
26. c
27. a
28. d
29. d
30. b
31. d
32. c
33. a
34. d
35. a
36. a
37. b
38. a
39. a
40. c
41. c
42. c
43. a
44. c
45. c
46. b
47. b
48. c
49. a
50. b
51. d
52. c
53. d
54. c
55. b
56. a
57. c
58. b
59. c
60. a

**America's Political
System at Work**
1. c
2. d
3. c
4. a

5. b
6. b
7. a
8. d
9. d
10. a
11. b
12. d
13. d
14. d

**Ideals of the
New Nation**
1. d
2. a
3. d
4. c
5. d
6. b
7. d
8. a
9. b
10. c
11. d
12. d
13. d
14. a
15. c

Foreign Policy
1. c
2. c
3. d
4. a
5. a
6. b
7. d
8. c
9. d
10. d
11. b
12. d
13. c

14. d
15. a
16. a
17. d
18. b
19. c

**Divergent Paths
of the Americans
The Northeasterners**
1. d
2. b
3. c
4. b
5. d
6. a
7. a
8. c
9. d
10. b
11. d
12. d
13. d
14. d
15. c

**Divergent Paths
of the Americans
The Southerners**
1. d
2. d
3. b
4. d
5. d
6. d
7. a
8. b
9. b
10. c
11. a

**Divergent Paths
of the Americans
The Westerners**

1. c
2. b
3. a
4. c
5. c
6. b
7. a
8. b
9. a
10. c
11. d
12. d
13. b
14. a
15. c
16. d
17. c
18. c

**The Abolitionist
Movement**

1. c
2. d
3. d
4. a
5. d
6. d
7. d
8. a
9. b
10. c
11. a
12. c
13. d
14. d
15. d
16. d
17. a

The Civil War

1. b
2. d
3. d

4. c
5. b
6. d
7. a
8. b
9. c
10. a
11. a
12. c
13. a
14. b
15. b
16. b
17. c
18. e
19. d
20. d
21. d
22. b
23. a
24. b
25. c
26. d
27. a
28. a
29. d
30. b
31. c
32. a
33. d
34. b
35. c

Reconstruction

1. d
2. c
3. a
4. d
5. b
6. a
7. c
8. a
9. d
10. a
11. b
12. c

13. d

**Industrial
Revolution**

1. a
2. c
3. a
4. c
5. d
6. b
7. a
8. c
9. e
10. d
11. a
12. b
13. c
14. d
15. b
16. a
17. d
18. d
19. c
20. b
21. c

SCIENCE

Content Cluster-PHYSICAL SCIENCE (Motion)

Objective: To learn the terminology and how to solve problems involving speed, distance, velocity, time, and distance

---

Parent Tip: The velocity of an object is the rate of change of its position. To describe the velocity of an object, one must specify both the direction and speed of the object. Changes in velocity can be the result of changes in speed, direction, or both. Acceleration is the rate of change of velocity. To determine acceleration one uses the formula $a = \frac{\Delta v}{t}$, where Δv is the change in velocity and t is the duration of time.

Choose the correct answer.

1. In order to determine a change in position or location, you need

    a. a reference point.
    b. a watch.
    c. a compass.
    d. a yard stick.

2. To measure the speed of an object you must measure

    a. the distance traveled by the object.
    b. the time it takes the object to travel the distance.
    c. the weight of the object.
    d. both a and b

3. When drawing a distance-time graph, one plots distance on the Y-axis. This is the

    a. horizontal axis of the graph.
    b. vertical axis of the graph.
    c. diagonal axis of the graph.
    d. lateral axis of the graph.

4. In the metric system, distance is measured in

    a. yards.
    b. miles.
    c. meters.
    d. feet.

5. In plotting a resting object on a distance-time graph, one would find

    a. a straight horizontal line at the bottom of the graph.
    b. a straight line drawn at a forty-five degree angle.
    c. a straight line drawn at a ninety degree angle.
    d. a S-shaped curved line.

6. Motion is

    a. a change in velocity.
    b. a change in speed.
    c. a change in position.
    d. a change in acceleration.

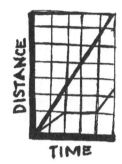

7. The speed of an object that does not vary is called

    a. instantaneous speed.
    b. average speed.
    c. constant speed.
    d. accelerated speed.

8. If a plane traveled 3600 miles in 6 hours, how many miles per hour is its speed?

    a. 300 miles/hour
    b. 360 miles/hour
    c. 600 miles/hour
    d. 1000 miles/hour

9. The problem with calculating the speed of an object simply by dividing distance by time is that

    a. it gives you an average speed, not the speed at various points.
    b. you need to divide time by the distance to get speed.
    c. all moving objects maintain a constant rate of speed.
    d. average speed only varies in the beginning of movement.

10. The term velocity is used to describe

    a. speed of an object without direction as a factor.
    b. direction of an object without speed as a factor.
    c. speed of an object in only terrestrial environments.
    d. the speed of an object in a given direction.

11. The rate of change in velocity and/or the change in direction is known as

    a. friction.
    b. acceleration.
    c. inertia.
    d. momentum.

12. How would the velocity of a person be determined if they were walking against the wind?

    a. The velocity of the wind would be subtracted from the velocity of the person walking normally.
    b. The velocity of the person walking normally would be added to the velocity of the wind.
    c. There would be no change in velocity regardless of walking against or with the wind.
    d. One could never determine velocity in this situation.

13. Find the velocity of a javelin that is thrown 50 meters in 5.5 seconds

    a. 4.20 meters/second
    b. 9.09 meters/second
    c. 10.65 meters/second
    d. 15.32 meters/second

14. How much time in seconds would it take an Olympic swimmer to swim the 100 meter freestyle at an average velocity of 2.05 meters/second?

    a. 20.50 seconds
    b. 41.25 seconds
    c. 48.78 seconds
    d. 62.05 seconds

15. Calculate the distance that a skateboarder can ride in 5 hours if the average speed was 12.1 miles/hour.

    a. 2.42 miles
    b. 24.2 miles
    c. 36.5 miles
    d. 60.5 miles

16. A fly ball hit by a baseball player is traveling at an average velocity of 12 meters/second. How far will the ball travel in 7.2 seconds?

    a. 55.4 meters
    b. 74.4 meters
    c. 86.4 meters
    d. 93.4 meters

17. The cities of Las Vegas, Nevada and Los Angeles, California are 275 miles apart. Approximately how long will it take to drive from one city to the other in a car travelling at 70 miles/hour?

    a. 3 hours
    b. 4 hours
    c. 5 hours
    d. 6 hours

18. Find the velocity of a cyclist that travels 250 meters in 12.2 seconds.

    a. 10.49 meters/second
    b. 20.49 meters/second
    c. 30.40 meters/second
    d. 35.49 meters/second

19. Acceleration is

    a. the rate at which velocity changes.
    b. sometimes a negative number.
    c. sometimes a positive number.
    d. all of the above

20. The velocity of a car changes from 39 meters/second to 0 meters/second as it approaches a stop sign. This change in velocity takes 13 seconds. Calculate the car's average acceleration.

    a. 2 meters/sec^2
    b. -2 meters/sec^2
    c. -3 meters/sec^2
    d. 3 meters/sec^2

21. As an airplane accelerates on the runway the velocity increases from 150 meters/second to 250 meters/second in 8 seconds. What is the average acceleration of the airplane?

    a. 3.74 meters/sec^2
    b. 4.74 meters/sec^2
    c. 7.69 meters/sec^2
    d. 12.5 meters/sec^2

22. Inertia is

    a. the tendency of an object to resist any change in its motion.
    b. the force of gravity that acts on a resting object.
    c. the effect of friction on a moving object.
    d. all of the above

23. Which of the following is part of Newton's Law of Motion?

    a. An object at rest will remain at rest unless acted upon by an unbalanced force.
    b. An object in motion will remain in motion at a constant velocity unless acted upon by an unbalanced force.
    c. For every action, there is an equal and opposite reaction.
    d. all of the above

24. A passenger in a car is involved in a head-on collision and is not wearing a seat belt. She continues to move forward and hits the windshield at the original velocity of the car because of

    a. acceleration.
    b. friction.
    c. inertia.
    d. the change of forces.

25. A metal weight is dropped from the third floor. When it hits the ground 2 seconds later, it has a velocity of 30 meters/second. What is the acceleration of the weight?

    a. 10 meters/sec^2
    b. 15 meters/sec^2
    c. 20 meters/sec^2
    d. 30 meters/sec^2

Content Cluster-PHYSICAL SCIENCE (Force)

Objective: To learn the physical concept of force and how unbalanced forces will cause an object to change velocity.

Parent Tip: Sir Isaac Newton created three laws to explain how forces are involved with motion. The first law is that an object moving at a constant velocity will keep moving at that velocity unless an unbalanced force is acted upon it. The second law states that the net force acting upon an object causes the object to accelerate in the direction of the force (force = mass x acceleration). The third law states that for every force placed upon an object, there is an equal and opposite reaction force.

---

1. A force

   a. is a push or a pull on an object.
   b. gives energy to an object.
   c. sometimes causes an object to move, stop, or change directions.
   d. all of the above

2. The SI unit (International System of Units) for force is called the

   a. pound.
   b. Newton.
   c. weight.
   d. mass.

3. When two forces are acting in the same direction, the total force is,

   a. one force subtracted from another.
   b. the two forces added together.
   c. zero, they cancel each other out.
   d. the two forces multiplied together.

4. Forces that are equal in size and opposite in direction are called

   a. unbalanced forces.
   b. net forces.
   c. balanced forces.
   d. gravitational force.

5. Newton's first law of motion states that if an object is at rest (not moving), it will stay at rest unless acted on by a

    a. unbalanced force.
    b. net force.
    c. balanced force.
    d. gravitational force.

6. An unseen force that will slow down or stop a moving object is called

    a. gravity.
    b. inertia.
    c. friction.
    d. momentum.

7. Which of the following has a force of friction?

    a. two solid objects in contact with each other
    b. air in contact with an object
    c. water in contact with an object
    d. all of the above

8. The force of friction between two objects in contact with each other is greatest when

    a. the surfaces of both objects are smooth.
    b. the surface of one object is smooth and the other is rough.
    c. the surfaces of both objects are rough.
    d. the surfaces of the objects are rounded.

9. To move an object that is sitting on the floor, one must apply a force that

    a. is equal to the force of friction.
    b. is greater than the force of friction.
    c. is greater than the mass of the object.
    d. is equal to the mass of the object.

10. The force of gravity acts upon all objects and is measured by

    a. mass.
    b. force.
    c. weight.
    d. volume.

11. A person that weighs 150 pounds on the Earth will weigh

    a. less on a larger planet such as Jupiter.
    b. more on the moon.
    c. less on a smaller planet such as Mars.
    d. the same on the moon and all planets.

12. As an object moves away from the center of the Earth, the force of gravity

    a. remains the same.
    b. increases.
    c. decreases.
    d. is reduced by half.

13. The quantity or amount of matter in an object is called the

    a. weight.
    b. mass.
    c. volume.
    d. texture.

14. The mass of a object that is 100 kg (kilograms) on the Earth will be

    a. more on a larger planet.
    b. less on a larger planet.
    c. more on the moon.
    d. the same everywhere because the mass of the object does not change.

15. The force of gravity between two objects depends upon

    a. their weights.
    b. their masses.
    c. the distance between them.
    d. b and c are correct

16. When an object falls to the ground, it is responding to the force of

    a. friction.
    b. gravity.
    c. resistance.
    d. space.

17. If the distance between the two objects is doubled, the force of attraction between them becomes 1/4 of what it was before. What will happen to the force if the distance is tripled?

    a. the force becomes 1/9 of the original force
    b. the force becomes 1/12 of the original force
    c. the force becomes 1/8 of the original force
    d. the force becomes three times the original force

18. The forces of gravity

    a. hold the Earth and the other planets in the solar system.
    b. give larger planets more gravitational pull than smaller planets.
    c. increase as the masses of the objects increase.
    d. all of the above

19. The planets revolves around the sun in an orbit and do not fly off into space because of

    a. the gravitational attraction between the sun and each planet.
    b. the rotation of each planet, which keeps them moving towards the sun.
    c. the magnetic attraction of negative and positive charges.
    d. the need for nine planets in our solar system for balance.

20. A Newton (N) is equal to which of the following expressions?

    a. $\dfrac{(kg)(meter)}{(sec^2)}$

    b. $(kg)(meter)(sec^2)$

    c. $\dfrac{(kg)(sec^2)}{(meter)}$

    d. $\dfrac{(meter)(sec^2)}{(kg)}$

21. What is the acceleration due to the force of gravity?

    a. 9.8 meters/sec^2
    b. $.98$ meters/sec^2
    c. 98 meters/sec^2
    d. 980 meters/sec^2

22. In throwing a baseball across the field, what are the forces involved as the ball travels through the air?

    a. the force carrying the ball forward (mass X acceleration)
    b. the force of gravity pulling the ball down
    c. the force of air friction slowing the ball down
    d. all of the above

23. What is the force needed to accelerate a car that has a mass of 950 kg, 2 meter/sec^2?

    a. 1900 newtons
    b. 475 newtons
    c. 950 newtons
    d. 2 newtons

24. A soccer ball is kicked with a force of 12 N (newtons). The ball has a mass of .30 kg (kilograms). What is the acceleration of the ball?

    a. 400 meters/sec^2
    b. 40 meters/sec^2
    c. 2.5 meters/sec^2
    d. 25 meters/sec^2

25. A snow machine is used to throw snow on a mountain with a force of 250N. The snow accelerates out of the machine at 5 meters/sec^2. What is the mass of the snow?

    a. 25 kg
    b. 2.5 kg
    c. 5.0 kg
    d. 50 kg

26. A 100 N force is applied to the right of a large crate. The reaction force will be

    a. 100 N to the right.
    b. 100 N to the left.
    c. 200 N to the right.
    d. 200 N to the left.

27. If gravity causes all falling objects to accelerate at 9.8 meters/sec^2, what would be the final velocity of a rock thrown off a bridge when it takes 5 seconds to reach the ground?

    a. 1.96 meters/sec
    b. 49 meters/sec
    c. 14.8 meters/sec
    d. 4.9 meters/sec

28. Anything that is thrown or shot through the air, is called a

    a. rocket.
    b. shuttle.
    c. projectile.
    d. spearhead.

Content Cluster-PHYSICAL SCIENCE (Structure of Matter)

Objective: To learn the properties and atomic structure of elements, the various states of matter, and how compounds are formed by combining elements

> **Parent Tip:** Matter is anything that takes up space. Atoms are found in all matter. These small structures are made of tiny particles (subatomic particles) some of which have charges on them. They combine to form compounds and mixtures and are found in substances that are liquid, solid, and gas. How closely the atoms are packed together and how fast the atoms are moving determine these three states of matter. The periodic table is the chart that is used to help identify some of the atoms called elements.

1. Which of the following is not one of the three common states of matter

   a. gas.
   b. liquid.
   c. solid.
   d. slush.

2. Size, shape, texture and color of a substance are examples of

   a. physical properties.
   b. chemical properties.
   c. bonding properties.
   d. subatomic properties.

3. Which of the following statements are true?

   a. When a substance has a change in its physical properties, it also changes its chemical properties.
   b. A substance can change its physical properties without changing its chemical properties.
   c. Physical properties describe how a substance acts when combined with other substances.
   d. Melting point, boiling points and freezing points are examples of chemical properties.

4. When the particles of a substance are held closely together and the substance has a definite shape and volume this is known as a

    a. gas.
    b. liquid.
    c. solid.
    d. plasma.

5. Matter that has no definite shape or volume is known as a

    a. gas.
    b. liquid.
    c. solid.
    d. plasma.

6. Which of the following are characteristics of a liquid?

    a. Particles have enough energy to move around each other.
    b. Has a definite volume.
    c. Assumes the shape of the container.
    d. all of the above

7. When the particles of a substance have enough energy to move quickly and overcome the attractive forces that hold them together, they expand to fill any volume. This is an example of a

    a. gas.
    b. liquid.
    c. solid.
    d. plasma.

8. A gas like mixture of positively and negatively charged particles that is the result of extremely high temperature is called plasma. Where is this state of matter found?

    a. the sun
    b. fluorescent light
    c. nebula
    d. all of the above

9. The most common state of matter in the universe is which of the following?

    a. gas
    b. liquid
    c. solid
    d. plasma

10. The energy needed to change a material from a liquid to a gas is called the heat of

    a. evaporation.
    b. condensation.
    c. vaporization.
    d. sublimation.

11. The energy needed to change a material from a solid to a liquid is called the heat of

    a. evaporation.
    b. fusion.
    c. vaporization.
    d. sublimation.

12. The change of a material from a solid phase directly to a gas phase (like dry ice) is called

    a. evaporation.
    b. fission.
    c. vaporization.
    d. sublimation.

13. Matter exists in which of the following

    a. mixtures.
    b. solutions.
    c. compounds and elements.
    d. all of the above

14. A mixture is

    a. when two or more different substances are mixed together but not combined chemically.
    b. when two or more substances are mixed together and combined chemically.
    c. the molecules of two or more different substances are mixed in the form of solutions, suspensions, and colloids.
    d. a and c are correct

15. A solution is a homogeneous mixture that is made of a

    a. solvent and a solute.
    b. positive and a negative ion.
    c. isotope.
    d. suspension and a colloid.

16. The solvent is a substance that dissolves other substances. The "universal solvent" is also known as

    a. an acid.
    b. water.
    c. a catalyst.
    d. a base.

17. The amount of solute that is dissolved in a given amount of solvent is called the

    a. saturation.
    b. suspension.
    c. concentration.
    d. chemical structure.

18. Which of the following is an example of a heterogeneous mixture called a suspension?

    a. a mixture that will separate in a short period of time
    b. oil and vinegar salad dressing
    c. dirt and water mixture
    d. all of the above

19. A colloid is a mixture in which the suspended particles are large and not dissolved. Unlike other suspensions however, they remain permanently suspended and do not separate. An example of this mixture is

    a. toothpaste.
    b. alcohol.
    c. ice tea.
    d. sea water.

20. The basic building blocks of all matter are

    a. cells.
    b. molecules.
    c. compounds.
    d. atoms.

21. Elements are substances

    a. that are the simplest pure substances.
    b. that cannot be changed into simpler substances by chemical means.
    c. that mostly occur naturally on the Earth.
    d. all of the above

22. The central core of an atom is called the

    a. brain.
    b. protocell.
    c. nucleus.
    d. proteus.

23. Which of the following subatomic particles have a positive charge

    a. neutron.
    b. electron.
    c. proton.
    d. none of the above

24. What is the charge found on the nucleus of an atom?

    a. negative
    b. positive
    c. no charge
    d. sometimes positive sometimes negative

25. Where are protons and neutrons found in the atom?

    a. Both are in the nucleus.
    b. Both orbit the nucleus.
    c. Protons are found in the nucleus and neutrons orbit the nucleus.
    d. Neutrons are found in the nucleus and protons orbit the nucleus.

26. Which of the subatomic particles have a negative charge?

    a. protons
    b. neutrons
    c. electrons
    d. none of these

27. Under certain conditions, an atom may gain or lose an electron.
    This atom is now (a) an

    a. ion.
    b. isotope.
    c. covalent molecule.
    d. polar molecule.

28. Which of the following are true?

    a. When an atom loses an electron it become negatively charged.
    b. When an atom loses an electron it becomes positively charged.
    c. When an atom gains an electron it becomes positively charged.
    d. all of the above

29. A chemical symbol represents what part of an element?

    a. its name
    b. its structure
    c. its chemical properties
    d. its type

30. A chemical property of a substance

    a. indicates whether it can undergo a certain chemical change.
    b. describes how a substance acts when it is combined with other substances.
    c. would include whether a substance is flammable or combustible.
    d. all of the above

31. The chart listing all of the elements according to their properties and increasing atomic number is called the

    a. ionic table.
    b. elemental table.
    c. periodic table.
    d. reactant table.

32. Two or more different elements that are chemically combined form a

    a. mixture.
    b. solution.
    c. compound.
    d. isotope.

33. The atomic number of an element will always tell you the number of

    a. protons found in the nucleus.
    b. electrons found in the element.
    c. neutrons found in the element.
    d. charges on the atom.

34. The properties of a compound are

   a. the same as the properties of the elements making up the compound.
   b. the same as the larger element making up the compound.
   c. the same as the smaller element making up the compound.
   d. different from the elements making up the compound.

35. A chemical symbol of an element

   a. consists of one or two letters.
   b. usually is taken from the elements name or Latin name.
   c. consists of a single capital letter or a capital letter and small case letter.
   d. all of the above

36. A specific element will always have the

   a. the same number of electrons.
   b. the same number of neutrons.
   c. the same number of protons.
   d. all of the above are correct

37. The number of atoms of each element in a molecule is indicated by the

   a. molecular formula.
   b. molecular weight.
   c. chemical bonds.
   d. chemical symbol.

38. An element that has a different number of neutrons is called (a) an

   a. ion.
   b. isotope.
   c. ionic compound.
   d. covalent compound.

39. In looking at the periodic table,

   a. the table consists of a box for each element.
   b. the elements are arranged in order by their atomic number.
   c. elements that are grouped together have similar properties.
   d. all of the above are correct

40. The elements grouped together in the far right column are called the noble gases. These gases

   a. are stable or unreactive.
   b. normally do not form compounds.
   c. are sometimes used in lights or to produce laser light shows.
   d. all of the above are correct

Content Cluster-EARTH SCIENCE (Earth and the Solar System)

Objective: To learn the structure and composition of the universe by studying stars, galaxies, planets, comets, asteroids and planetary satellites (moons).

Parent Tip: Our planet, Earth is just a small part of the expanding structure called the universe. Nine planets including Earth form the solar system and are part of the Milky Way galaxy. There are an uncountable number of galaxies in the universe, each with billions of stars, including our sun that provides light. These galaxies and the stars within them are vast distances apart measured in terms of the speed of light. The stars are created and eventually burn out in a predictable pattern. Included in our solar system are comets, asteroids, and meteoroids.

Choose the correct answer.

1. By the term universe, scientists mean

   a. all the material in outer space.
   b. everything physical including matter and energy that exists in space and time.
   c. all of the solar systems in our galaxy.
   d. the constellations and stars in the sky.

2. A collection of stars, nebulae, gases, dust, and planets is called a

   a. solar system.
   b. galaxy.
   c. black hole.
   d. constellation.

3. The theory for the origin of the universe is called the

   a. biogenesis theory.
   b. big bang theory.
   c. doppler theory.
   d. black hole theory.

4. The name of the galaxy that we live in is called the

   a. Milky Way Galaxy.
   b. Magellanic Galaxy.
   c. Supernova Galaxy.
   d. Andromeda Galaxy.

5. Which of the following is included in the major classes of galaxies?

    a. elliptical
    b. spiral
    c. irregular
    d. all of the above

6. Which of the following forces holds galaxies together?

    a. frictional forces
    b. gravitational forces
    c. electrical forces
    d. mechanical forces

7. Which of the following describes the most common type of galaxy found in the universe?

    a. spherical or football shaped ellipses
    b. spiral with arms winding outward from inner regions
    c. smaller irregular shaped with little dust and gas
    d. all of the above

8. Galaxies are not spread out evenly throughout the universe. They are grouped together in

    a. clusters.
    b. constellations.
    c. local groups.
    d. solar systems.

9. The creation of the universe by the big bang theory is supported by

    a. the Doppler shift to red.
    b. the Doppler shift to blue.
    c. the Doppler shift to yellow.
    d. the Doppler shift to green.

10. Evidence from scientific study indicates that the universe

    a. is condensing.
    b. is expanding.
    c. is breaking into small pieces.
    d. is merging into one body.

11. Matter that is so massive and compressed that nothing, not even light, can escape its gravitational field is called

    a. supernova.
    b. white dwarf.
    c. neutron star.
    d. black hole.

12. To measure distances in the universe beyond Earth, scientists use the term

    a. light-year.
    b. megamile.
    c. stardate.
    d. warp-year.

13. Patterns of stars in the sky first described by the Greeks are called

    a. dippers.
    b. constellations.
    c. star clusters.
    d. nebulae.

14. A stars brightness is called its

    a. color index.
    b. magnitude.
    c. intensity.
    d. wavelength.

15. What causes the appearance of change in the position of the constellations throughout the year?

    a. The Earth revolving around the stars in the galaxy.
    b. The Earth revolving around the sun.
    c. The sun revolving around the stars in the galaxy.
    d. The universe expanding.

16. The color of a star is related to its

    a. temperature.
    b. density.
    c. size.
    d. position in space.

17. Stars like the sun, produce energy by

    a. fusing hydrogen atoms into helium.
    b. splitting water.
    c. condensing a cloud of gas and dust.
    d. splitting atoms.

18. The hottest stars in the universe are which color?

    a. red
    b. yellow
    c. blue
    d. white

19. The coolest stars in the universe are which color?

    a. red
    b. yellow
    c. blue
    d. white

20. Stars begin their life

    a. as great clouds of gas and dust called nebula.
    b. with different masses.
    c. with different life expectancies.
    d. all of the above

21. Most of the stars in the universe including the sun are

    a. main-sequence stars.
    b. red-giant stars.
    c. supernova.
    d. white dwarf stars.

22. What happens to the main-sequence stars just before they die?

    a. They become red-giant stars and expand.
    b. They become brighter supernovas.
    c. They become black holes absorbing all matter.
    d. They become supergiants with great gravitational forces.

23. A light-year is

    a. the distance light travels in one year.
    b. 9.5×10^{15} meters.
    c. the distance that a car would travel a highway speed in 10 million years.
    d. all of the above

24. The sequence of life to death of our star the sun is which of the following

    a. nebula, high-mass star, supergiant, supernova, black hole.
    b. nebula, high-mass star, red giant, white dwarf, black hole.
    c. nebula, low-mass star, red giant, white dwarf, black dwarf.
    d. nebula, low-mass star, supergiant, supernova, white dwarf.

25. The brighter the star

    a. the larger the magnitude.
    b. the smaller the magnitude.
    c. the smaller the wavelength.
    d. the larger the wavelength.

26. Which is the fourth planet from the sun, smaller than the Earth, with two moons?

    a. Mercury
    b. Venus
    c. Mars
    d. Uranus

27. An icy object that travels around the sun in an elliptical orbit is called a

    a. comet.
    b. meteorite.
    c. asteroid.
    d. supernova.

28. The planet found nearest to the sun and does not have an atmosphere is

    a. Mercury.
    b. Mars.
    c. Neptune.
    d. Uranus.

29. An natural orbiting satellite around a planet is called a

    a. moon.
    b. comet.
    c. star.
    d. meteor.

30. A chunk of rock or metal that is in orbit around the sun and sometimes collides with the Earth is called

    a. comet.
    b. meteoroid.
    c. asteroid.
    d. supernova.

31. The second planet from the sun that resembles Earth in size, mass and density is

    a. Mars.
    b. Venus.
    c. Neptune.
    d. Uranus.

32. The smallest planet in our solar system with a moon about half its size is called

    a. Mercury.
    b. Mars.
    c. Pluto.
    d. Earth.

33. The tail of a comet is cause by

    a. the heat of the sun .
    b. the refraction of light.
    c. the gravity of Earth.
    d. the gravity of the sun.

34. The third planet from the sun, that has an atmosphere of oxygen, nitrogen and hydrogen and one orbiting moon is called

    a. Mars.
    b. Venus.
    c. Earth.
    d. Mercury.

35. When a meteoroid does not complete burn up as it passes through the Earth's atmosphere,

    a. it impacts the Earth surface as a meteorite.
    b. it is seen as a shooting star.
    c. it can create a large and deep crater in the Earth.
    d. all of the above

36. Which is the large planet that has at least twenty-three moons and a spectacular ring system?

    a. Saturn
    b. Jupiter
    c. Uranus
    d. Neptune

37. Irregularly shaped bodies that revolve around the sun in an area between Mars and Jupiter are called

    a. comets.
    b. meteoroids.
    c. asteroids.
    d. supernovas.

38. The largest planet in our solar system that has sixteen moons and is composed of hydrogen and helium gas is called

    a. Saturn.
    b. Jupiter.
    c. Neptune.
    d. Uranus.

39. The order of the planets starting with Mercury closest to the sun is

    a. Mercury, Earth, Mars, Venus, Saturn, Jupiter, Neptune, Uranus, Pluto.
    b. Mercury, Mars, Earth, Venus, Saturn, Jupiter, Uranus, Neptune, Pluto.
    c. Mercury, Venus, Earth, Mars, Jupiter, Saturn, Uranus, Neptune, Pluto.
    d. Mercury, Mars, Earth, Venus, Jupiter, Saturn, Uranus, Neptune, Pluto.

40. Jupiter, Saturn, Uranus, and Neptune are known as

    a. the inner planets.
    b. the terrestrial planets.
    c. the Jovian planets.
    d. the ringed planets.

41. The third largest planet, with 15 moons and an atmosphere of methane gas is called

    a. Saturn.
    b. Uranus.
    c. Neptune.
    d. Pluto.

42. The eighth planet from the sun that is composed of water, ammonia, and molten rock is called

    a. Saturn.
    b. Uranus.
    c. Neptune.
    d. Pluto.

43. The satellites that orbit the Jovian planets

    a. are over 40 in number.
    b. are made of rock and/or ice.
    c. include many that are as large or larger than the Earth.
    d. all of the above are correct

44. Planets

    a. reflect light from the sun.
    b. reflect the light from other planets.
    c. give off there own light.
    d. are illuminated by the other stars in the solar system.

45. Which of following planets are called the terrestrial planets because of their composition?

    a. Mercury, Mars, Earth, and Neptune
    b. Mercury, Mars, Jupiter, and Saturn
    c. Mars, Venus, Neptune, and Uranus
    d. Mercury, Mars, Venus, and Earth

46. Stars are formed by

    a. nebula collecting dust and gas as it travels through space.
    b. the large mass of the nebula attracting more matter.
    c. gravity pulling the dust, gas, and matter tightly together.
    d. all of the above

Cluster Content-PHYSICAL SCIENCE (Reactions)

Objective: To learn the processes of chemical reactions and provide an understanding of chemical properties such as freezing, boiling, heat production, and pH.

Parent Tip: Reacting atoms and molecules form products with different chemical properties. However, in chemical reactions the number of atoms and the mass of the substances will always stay the same. Chemical reactions usually liberate or absorb heat. By adding or removing heat energy, the physical characteristics of a substance, including its form of being a liquid, solid, or gas, can change. One important tool to determine whether a solution is an acid, base, or neutral (as in pure water) is the pH test.

Choose the correct answer.

1. The description of a chemical reaction using chemical symbols and formulas is called

    a. a chemical equation.
    b. a reaction statement.
    c. a chemical summery.
    d. a chemical inventory.

2. Chemical reactions occur when

    a. any two substances come in contact with each other.
    b. substances undergo chemical changes to form new substances.
    c. substances undergo a change in their physical characteristics.
    d. water is added to any substance.

3. Which of the following are signs that a chemical reaction is taking place

    a. a change in color.
    b. a release of gas.
    c. the production of heat.
    d. all of the above

4. Chemical equations are balanced because of the

    a. law of conservation of mass.
    b. law of conservation of energy.
    c. associative law of addition.
    d. distributive law of multiplication.

5. Chemical reactions that release energy are called

    a. exothermic.
    b. endothermic.
    c. endergonic.
    d. both b and c are correct

6. Substances that prevent chemical reactions are called

    a. catalysts.
    b. inhibitors.
    c. reactants.
    d. radicals.

7. The energy that is required to start a reaction is called

    a. activation energy.
    b. potential energy.
    c. solar energy.
    d. light energy.

8. In a chemical reaction the arrow points to the substances called

    a. reactants.
    b. products.
    c. enzymes.
    d. coefficients.

9. A substance that speeds up a reaction without being used itself is called

    a. a reactant.
    b. a product.
    c. a catalyst.
    d. energy.

10. The term that means "to make" or "to build" is

    a. combustion.
    b. decomposition.
    c. synthesis.
    d. displacement.

11. Decomposition reactions

    a. join smaller molecules to make larger molecules.
    b. are reactions in which materials are broken apart.
    c. require oxygen.
    d. do not include digestion.

12. Synthesis reactions

    a. always join substances.
    b. have a product that is a more complex compound than the reactants.
    c. include photosynthesis.
    d. all of the above

13. A reaction where one element replaces another in a compound is called a

    a. double-displacement reaction.
    b. synthesis reaction.
    c. combustion reaction.
    d. single-displacement reaction.

14. The reaction represented by the equation $AB + CD \rightarrow AD + CB$, AB and CD are the

    a. products.
    b. reactants.
    c. catalysts.
    d. inhibitors.

15. The reaction represented by the equation $AB + CD \rightarrow AD + CB$ is a

    a. synthesis reaction.
    b. decomposition reaction.
    c. single-displacement reaction.
    d. double-displacement reaction.

16. The law of conservation of mass states

    a. the starting mass of the reactants equals the final mass of the products.
    b. the starting mass of the reactants is greater than the final mass of the products.
    c. the starting mass of the reactants is less than the final mass of the products.
    d. the starting mass of the reactants has no relationship to the final mass of the products.

17. Which of the following is a balanced chemical equation?

    a. $2H_2O \rightarrow 2H_2 + O_2$
    b. $AgNO_3 + 2NaCl \rightarrow AgCl + NaNO_3$
    c. $6 CO_2 + 6H_2O \rightarrow C_6H_{12}O_6 + O_2$
    d. $Al + O_2 \rightarrow Al_2O_3$

18. In balancing chemical equations, one must

    a. have the same number of atoms of each element on each side of the equation.
    b. never change the subscripts of a correct chemical formula.
    c. balance the reactants with the products.
    d. all of the above

19. Energy is always involved in a chemical reaction. The energy absorbed or released is usually in the form of

    a. heat or light.
    b. friction.
    c. gas.
    d. a liquid.

20. The activation energy that is required for the start of an endergonic reaction is usually in the form of

    a. light.
    b. water.
    c. heat.
    d. pressure.

21. Because energy content is an important factor for the different phases of matter

    a. substances can be made to change phases by adding energy.
    b. substances can be made to change phases by removing energy.
    c. phase changes can be made by heating or cooling a substance.
    d. all of the above

22. Melting is

    a. changing a liquid to a solid.
    b. changing a solid to a gas.
    c. changing a solid to a liquid.
    d. changing a liquid to a gas.

23. The temperature that changes a liquid to a solid is called the

    a. freezing point.
    b. melting point.
    c. boiling point.
    d. condensation point.

24. The boiling point of a liquid

    a. changes with the volume of material.
    b. changes with the size of the container.
    c. decreases when the air pressure above the liquid is reduced.
    d. decreases when the air pressure above the liquid is increase.

25. When a solid changes directly into a gas, this is called

    a. evaporation.
    b. sublimation.
    c. vaporization.
    d. boiling.

26. In pure water

    a. the hydrogen ions are greater than the hydroxide ions.
    b. the hydroxide ions are greater than the hydrogen ions.
    c. the hydrogen ions are equal to the hydroxide ions.
    d. there are no hydroxide ions.

27. Acids are compounds that

    a. release hydrogen ions in water.
    b. release hydroxide ions in water.
    c. release hydrogen and hydroxide ions in water.
    d. all of the above are correct

28. The pH number of a acid is a number

    a. equal to 7.
    b. greater than then the number 7.
    c. less than the number 7.
    d. that is negative.

29. Bases are compounds that

    a. release hydrogen ions in water.
    b. release hydroxide ions in water.
    c. have a pH number less than 7.
    d. turn blue litmus paper red.

30 The pH scale

    a. measures the concentration of hydronium ions.
    b. ranges from numbers from 0-14.
    c. has neutral solution at a value of 7.
    d. all of the above are correct.

31. Acid solutions

    a. have a pH greater than 7 and turn blue litmus paper red.
    b. have a pH less than 7 and turn red litmus paper blue.
    c. have a pH less than 7 and turn blue litmus paper red.
    d. have a pH less than 7 and turns blue litmus paper green.

32. A solution that has a pH of 7

    a. is neutral.
    b. can be pure water.
    c. has equal amounts of hydrogen and hydroxide ions.
    d. all of the above are correct

Cluster Content-LIFE SCIENCE (Chemistry of Living Systems)

Objective: To learn the principles of chemistry involved with functional biological systems.

Parent Tip: There are many different molecules and elements found on the Earth. Some of these materials are essential for living things to survive. The two major groups of molecules found on the Earth are called inorganic compounds and organic compounds. The most important inorganic compound is water. Many of the inorganic elements are necessary for living things to make vital organic compounds. The major organic compounds are the carbohydrates (the energy source), the proteins (the building material), lipids (insulation and hormones), and nucleic acids (genetics and control of the cells).

Choose the correct answer.

1. Of the ninety naturally occurring element on the Earth which of the following are the six essential elements for living organisms?

   a. carbon, iron, hydrogen, sodium, lead, and mercury
   b. carbon, oxygen, nitrogen, gold, silver, and helium
   c. carbon, hydrogen, nitrogen, oxygen, phosphorus, and sulfur
   d. carbon, hydrogen, nitrogen, oxygen, water, and iron

2. The element carbon is important to living organisms because

   a. it can bond with other carbons atoms as well as many other elements.
   b. it can form straight chains, branched chains, or rings.
   c. it can bond with up to four atoms at once.
   d. all of the above are correct

3. A compound that is made by a living organism and contains the element carbon is called a (an)

   a. inorganic compound.
   b. organic compound.
   c. polar compound.
   d. ionic compound.

4. The most common organic compounds are

   a. carbohydrates and proteins.
   b. lipids and nucleic acids.
   c. water and salt.
   d. both a and b are correct

5. The element nitrogen is important in the formation of

   a. fats.
   b. carbohydrates.
   c. proteins.
   d. all of the above are correct

6. The element phosphorus is important in making

   a. nucleic acid and ATP (an energy compound).
   b. sugar.
   c. protein.
   d. fat.

7. Most organic molecules are constructed of basic units that are continuously repeated. These units are called

   a. polymers.
   b. monomers.
   c. isomers.
   d. dicots.

8. The building material of all living things is called

   a. protein.
   b. fats.
   c. carbohydrates.
   d. nucleic acids.

9. The process of combining two monomers together to form a larger molecule is called

   a. dehydration synthesis.
   b. oxidation.
   c. hydrolysis.
   d. polymerization.

10. The nucleic acids are

   a. citric acid and amino acid.
   b. DNA and RNA.
   c. stomach acid and boric acid.
   d. all of the above are correct

11. Another name for dehydration synthesis is

    a. digestion.
    b. oxidation.
    c. condensation reaction.
    d. reduction.

12. The condensation of many monomers produces a complex molecule called a

    a. isomer.
    b. isotope.
    c. polymer.
    d. nucleus.

13. The monomer that makes up all carbohydrates is called a

    a. polysaccharide.
    b. disaccharide.
    c. trisaccharide.
    d. monosaccharide.

14. Proteins are made up of many

    a. carbohydrates.
    b. nucleic acids.
    c. amino acids.
    d. fatty acids.

15. The most common monosaccharide that is used by living things as an energy source
    is called

    a. starch.
    b. glycerin.
    c. glucose.
    d. glycogen.

16. Water is an important inorganic material required by all living organisms. Which of
    the following properties are important for living things?

    a. water resists temperature change
    b. water is an excellent solvent
    c. water serves as an internal means of transportation
    d. all of the above are correct

17. Lipids are fats, oils, and waxes. The most common type of lipid is made of

    a. glycerol and three fatty acids.
    b. glucose and protein.
    c. carbohydrates and unsaturated acids.
    d. nucleic acids and protein.

18. The breaking down of large polymers to smaller molecules that can be used by living organisms is called

    a. condensation.
    b. hydrolysis.
    c. dehydration.
    d. replication.

19. Sugar is stored in animals as which of the following compounds?

    a. cellulose
    b. starch
    c. fat
    d. glycogen

20. Enzymes are important compounds that help to speed up chemical reactions in living organisms. Enzymes are made of what important material?

    a. carbohydrates
    b. lipids
    c. proteins
    d. nucleic acids

21. Organism are made of many different molecules. Which is the one molecule found in the greatest percentage?

    a. protein
    b. sugar
    c. water
    d. DNA

22. Amino acids are joined by special bonds to form proteins. These bonds are called

    a. enzyme bonds.
    b. ionic bonds.
    c. peptide bonds.
    d. polar bonds.

Content Cluster-PHYSICAL SCIENCE (Periodic Table)

Objective: To learn the organization of the periodic table, identify the regions of the table corresponding to metals, non-metals, and inert gases, and to understand chemical terms including atomic number, mass number, hardness, and electrical conductivity.

> **Parent Tip:** To help the student learn about the periodic table, it is suggested that one be obtained to study the various groups and locations. While it not necessary to memorize every symbol and member of each group, it is important to learn the general location of the metals, non-metals, and gases on the periodic table and have a general knowledge of the similar characteristics that are observed in the members of each group.

Using the Periodic Table on page 222, choose the best answer.

1. In the periodic table, the columns of elements are called families or groups. Elements within a family

   a. have similar but not identical properties.
   b. have the same number of electrons.
   c. have the same number of neutrons.
   d. have the same number of protons.

2. The horizontal rows of the periodic table are called

   a. groups.
   b. clans.
   c. periods.
   d. partners.

3. The noble gases are in group 18 on the far right side of the table and are stable and inert (unreactive). They include

   a. Helium.
   b. Neon.
   c. Argon.
   d. all of the above are correct

4. The rows of the periodic table are organized with

   a. the number of protons and electrons in each element increasing by one as you move from left to right.
   b. the number of protons and electrons in each element decreasing by one as you move left to right.
   c. the negative charge on the atom increasing by one as you move left to right.
   d. the positive charge on the atom increasing by one as you move left to right.

5. The top number in each box is

    a. the mass number, indicating the number of protons in the element.
    b. the atomic number, indicating the number of protons in the element.
    c. the mass number, indicating the number of neutrons in the element.
    d. the atomic number, indicating the number of neutrons in the element.

6. Group 1 on the periodic table is the far left side column and are

    a. the alkali metals.
    b. the alkaline metals.
    c. the transition metals.
    d. the non-metals.

7. The bottom number in each box is the

    a. the mass number, indicating the total number of protons and neutrons in the nucleus of the element.
    b. the atomic number, indicating the total number of protons and neutrons in the nucleus of the element.
    c. the mass number, indicating the total number of electrons in the element.
    d. the atomic number, indicating the total number of electrons in the element .

8. Alkali metals are

    a. soft and shiny.
    b. highly reactive.
    c. found in nature as compounds with other elements.
    d. all of the above are correct

9. The alkaline-earth metals are found in

    a. the middle of the periodic table.
    b. in the column on the far right side of the periodic table.
    c. in the second column from the left of the periodic table.
    d. on the bottom row of the periodic table.

10. The alkaline-earth metals are less reactive than the alkali metals and include

    a. Calcium, Magnesium, and Barium.
    b. Iron, Silver, and Gold.
    c. Tin, Lead, and Copper.
    d. Zinc, Platinum, and Nickel.

11. Transition metals are found groups 3 through 12 on the periodic table. These metals

    a. have properties different than any other families.
    b. are sometimes used in jewelry.
    c. are often used in electrical wiring.
    d. all of the above are correct

12. Which of the following are the best conductors of heat and electricity?

    a. metals
    b. non-metals
    c. halogens
    d. noble gases

13. Which of the following groups are explosive when mixed with water?

    a. transitional metals
    b. alkali metals
    c. halogens
    d. alkaline metals

14. Which group of elements are dull in appearance, brittle and powdery?

    a. the solid non-metals
    b. the transitional metals
    c. the halogens
    d. the noble gases

15. The non metals are on the right side of the periodic table and include

    a. the top element in group 13 and top two elements in group 14.
    b. the top three elements in group 15 and the top four element is group 16.
    c. all of the elements in group 17 and group 18.
    d. all of the above are correct

Periodic Table of the Elements

Cluster Content-PHYSICAL SCIENCE (Density and Buoyancy)

Objective: To learn the concepts of two physical properties of matter, density and buoyancy.

> **Parent Tip:** The density of an object is the amount of mass contained in a given volume. It is calculated by dividing the mass of an object by the volume. The mass of the object will need to be in grams (g) and the volume in cubic centimeters (cm³). Density is important because it allow you to compare different types of material. The densities of many materials are recorded and charted to help in identifying unknown substances. The density of a material in comparison to water will determine whether it will float or sink.

Choose the correct answer.

1. Matter is anything that has

    a. mass.
    b. density.
    c. volume.
    d. all of the above are correct

2. Density is the

    a. mass divide by the volume.
    b. volume divide by the mass.
    c. the mass times the volume.
    d. the volume divided by the mass.

3. Volume is the amount of space in which an object exists. The metric units used to describe volume is the

    a. ounce and pound.
    b. quart and gallon.
    c. liter and cubic centimeter.
    d. meter and yard.

4. 1 cubic centimeter (cm³) is equal to

    a. 1 liter (1L).
    b. 1 milliliter (1ml).
    c. 10 milliliters (10ml).
    d. 10 liters (10L).

5. If the density of aluminum is 2.7 g/cm^3 and the density of silver is 10.5 g/cm^3 and you have a 5 cm^3 cube of a shiny metal weighing 52.5 grams, which metal is this?

   a. aluminum
   b. silver
   c. neither aluminum or silver
   d. a mixture of both metals

6. If the density of iron is 7.86 g/cm^3, what would be the mass of an iron rod whose volume is 30 cm^3?

   a. 3.82 grams
   b. 26.2 grams
   c. 235.8 grams
   d. 382.0 grams

7. If you have a bar of gold, a bar of lead, and a bar of silver of the same volume and you know the density of gold is 19.3, lead is 11.3 and silver is 10.5. What is the order from the heaviest to the lightest?

   a. silver, lead, gold
   b. gold, lead silver
   c. gold, silver, lead
   d. silver, gold, lead

8. A piece of metal has a volume of 8.4 cm^3 and a mass of 92.8 grams. What is the density of the metal?

   a. 11.05 g/cm^3
   b. 90.50 g/cm^3
   c. 110.5 g/cm^3
   d. 9.05 g/cm^3

9. The density of fresh water is 1g/ml or 1g/cm^3. Any material that has a density greater than 1g/ml will

   a. float on fresh water.
   b. sink in fresh water.
   c. float only if the volume of the water is twice the volume of the material.
   d. float only if the volume of the material is twice the volume of the water.

10. The buoyant force on an object in a fluid is an upward force equal to the weight of the fluid it has displaced. This is

    a. Archimedes' principle.
    b. Pascal's principle.
    c. Bernoulli's principle.
    d. none of the above

11. The amount of buoyant force will determine

    a. whether an object can float or sink in a fluid.
    b. whether an object is more dense than a fluid.
    c. the volume of the fluid need to float an object.
    d. the density of the water.

12. An object will float in a fluid when

    a. it displaces a volume of fluid whose weight is greater than the object's weight.
    b. it displaces a volume of fluid whose weight is equal to the object's weight.
    c. the density of the object is less than that of the fluid.
    d. all of the above are correct

SCIENCE
Answer Key

Motion
1. a
2. d
3. b
4. c
5. a
6. c
7. c
8. c
9. a
10. d
11. b
12. a
13. b
14. c
15. d
16. c
17. b
18. b
19. d
20. c
21. d
22. a
23. d
24. c
25. b

Force
1. d
2. b
3. b
4. c
5. a
6. c
7. d
8. c
9. b
10. c
11. c
12. c
13. b
14. d

15. d
16. b
17. a
18. d
19. a
20. a
21. a
22. a
23. a
24. b
25. d
26. b
27. b
28. c

Structure of Matter
1. d
2. a
3. b
4. c
5. a
6. d
7. a
8. d
9. d
10. c
11. b
12. d
13. d
14. d
15. a
16. b
17. c
18. d
19. a
20. d
21. d
22. c
23. c
24. b
25. a

26. c
27. a
28. b
29. a
30. d
31. c
32. c
33. a
34. d
35. d
36. c
37. a
38. b
39. d
40. d

Solar System
1. b
2. b
3. b
4. a
5. d
6. b
7. a
8. a
9. a
10. b
11. d
12. a
13. b
14. b
15. b
16. a
17. a
18. c
19. a
20. d
21. a
22. a
23. d
24. c

25. b
26. c
27. a
28. a
29. a
30. b
31. b
32. c
33. a
34. c
35. d
36. a
37. c
38. b
39. c
40. c
41. b
42. c
43. d
44. a
45. d
46. d

Reactions
1. a
2. b
3. d
4. a
5. a
6. b
7. a
8. b
9. c
10. c
11. b
12. d
13. d
14. b
15. d
16. a
17. a
18. d

19. a
20. c
21. d
22. c
23. a
24. c
25. b
26. c
27. a
28. c
29. b
30. d
31. c
32. d

Chemistry of Living Things
1. c
2. d
3. b
4. d
5. c
6. a
7. b
8. a
9. a
10. b
11. c
12. c
13. d
14. c
15. c
16. d
17. a
18. b
19. d
20. c
21. c
22. c

Periodic Table
1. a
2. c
3. d
4. a

5. b
6. a
7. a
8. d
9. c
10. a
11. d
12. a
13. b
14. a
15. d

Density and Buoyancy
1. d
2. a
3. c
4. b
5. b
6. c
7. b
8. a
9. b
10. a
11. a
12. d

NOTES